CHILDREN'S OBJECT LESSON SERMONS

Jim and Doris Morentz

Based on the
Common Lectionary Year B

Abingdon Press • Nashville

CHILDREN'S OBJECT LESSON SERMONS
BASED ON THE COMMON LECTIONARY YEAR B

Library of Congress Cataloging in Publication Data

MORENTZ, JIM.
    Children's object lesson sermons.
    1. Children's sermons. 2. Christian education—
Audio-visual aids.
    I. Morentz, Doris, 1929-   . II. Title.
BV4315.M627   1984   252'.53   84-10986

ISBN 0-687-06499-6

Scripture quotations unless otherwise noted are from the
Revised Standard Version Common Bible, copyright © 1973 by
the Division of Christian Education of the National Council of
Churches in the U.S.A., and are used by permission.

MANUFACTURED BY THE PARTHENON PRESS AT
NASHVILLE, TENNESSEE, UNITED STATES OF AMERICA

Dedication

To
Jim and Deb—who taught us everything we know about children, especially the joys of being parents.

And to
Our grandchildren—who taught us what only grandparents know, it *is* different the second time around. Emily, who came from Korea in September 1979, and Andy, born February 1980, children of Jim, and Christopher, born to Deb in September 1983.

Contents

Introduction

W e are amazed how much children can understand on a level higher than we normally give
them credit or opportunity to prove. This book of object
lesson sermons affords the opportunity for children to
be challenged to learn while they are having fun in their
special part of the service.

All of the sermons in this book are included in a series.
Most match the church season; some may have two or
three series in one season. Prior to each series there is an
introduction to help you understand what is coming.
There is also a list of the objects that will be used, so that
you can plan ahead. Each sermon has a key word, a vital
part of the sermon and the year-long learning process.
Occasionally at the bottom of the introduction page
there will be an advance notice about the next series.
Watch for these; your job will be made easier by them.
That is the whole idea of this book.

Suggestions on
How to Use This Book

This book should make life a little easier for you this year. If it does not, then we have failed in one of our goals. Let's say you are a busy person, you approve of children's sermons, but to create fifty-five sermons a year is not your cup of tea. This book has done that for you. Do not let these sermons be a straitjacket each Sunday, but rather a springboard that triggers your imagination and makes the sermon reflect your personal touch, which brings it to life in your situation. The children should learn and have fun. As you present the sermons, there will be ample opportunity for you to make a lot of discoveries together. In order for both of you to have fun, you must be prepared.

Use the key word as your sermon title. List the title in the bulletin; it will show, to the surprise of parents, that you consider these sermons important and that you do plan ahead. If you list a sermon series for a certain season in your parish paper, include the list of children's sermons also. It will again show the importance and planning you put into these sermons.

All of these sermons are nearly perfect. They only need your thorough preparation and personal touch to make them perfect. Good luck, on achieving perfection this year.

Notice: It has come to our attention that some pastors enlist a lay person to assist them in procuring the objects. This is a terrific idea if you can find a dependable person, one who enjoys this kind of treasure hunt. Give that person the list of objects required a month in advance, and request that they be delivered to you a week before the series starts. What a joy for a person who will do this, what a load off your mind!

Advent

(*Four Sundays*)

T he four Sundays of Advent will be a celebration of the four seasons of the year: spring, summer, fall, winter. The objects may vary somewhat, depending on where you live. This will be true of a few words in the sermons. This is a look at the year to come in the first four Sundays of the church year.

The subtle theme of the Advent series is to convey the idea that the year is divided into seasons that they all know. Now they will discover that the church year is divided into seasons also.

Objects Required
☆ flowers (altar flowers can be used)
☆ bathing suit
☆ football
☆ glove or another piece of winter clothing

First Sunday in Advent

Gospel Lesson: Mark 13:32-37
Key Word: **Spring**
Object: Flowers

I t is a new year again in the church. This is the first Sunday in Advent and the first day of the church year. The Advent season is the four weeks before Christmas. For the next four Sundays we are going to talk about the seasons of the year: spring, summer, fall, winter. We will be going through a whole year in just four short weeks.

Which one of the seasons shall we start with today, the first day of the new year? *Spring* is our word for today. We watch for that first sign of spring. If you live where it is cold or it snows, you look for a crocus or a daffodil bud. In the West or Southwest you watch for the hills to turn brown. If you live in the warm South you look for the trees to blossom. Wherever we live we look for that new life that we know spring brings.

Do you remember when spring begins? It starts on the same date each year—March 21. But that is just a date on the calendar. The signs we look for sometimes come early, sometimes late, then again sometimes right on time.

That is what our Gospel lesson was about this morning. Not when will spring come, but when will God come. He will come but we don't know when; like spring he may be early, he may be late, but you have to be ready for his coming.

Prepare the garden. Put on lime and fertilizer and check the bulbs that have been sleeping in the ground since they last bloomed. Get everything ready, because if you do not work to get things in good shape, your garden will not be ready to bloom and welcome spring.

If you do the right things, you can sit and watch and wait to see the flowers pop out of the ground and bloom in all their glory. (Hold up flowers.)

Mark tells us the same thing in the story today. Watch! Be ready! Do not be caught unprepared. Spring just suddenly seems to happen. Unless you have prepared for spring or God, you won't be ready. Be prepared, watch, do not be caught sleeping.

Second Sunday in Advent

Gospel Lesson: Mark 1:1-8
Key Word: **Summer**
Object: A bathing suit

T oday in our discussion about the seasons we put emphasis on our key word *summer.* Our Gospel today introduces us to John the Baptist. That is what he is usually called, but today Mark calls him John the Baptizer, because that is his mission.

John the Baptist had some good days and some bad ones. This is one of John's good days. He is out in the wilderness, preaching and baptizing many.

It is a kind of survival camp where you are out in the country and your camp is set up and you just live off the land. You eat berries, you may even find honey, and there are plants that are good to eat also. It is a lot of fun and an experience you will not forget since you will prove to yourself that you can survive in the wilds.

For my outing this summer I brought along a bathing suit. (Hold up suit.) I am going to be ready to take a swim in case there is a pond or a river like the River Jordan where John the Baptist camped.

At this point in John's wilderness ministry things seemed to be going great. The Gospel says all the people went to hear him preach and to be baptized.

Oh, things went great and the time just flew by. You know how that is, when school is out for the summer, you have so much fun you hope summer never ends. Then, finally, you start to get a little tired of the summer, and you can hardly believe it, but you say to yourself, "I wonder when school starts?"

Some of you I know wish your summer vacation would never end. I can understand that, but it always does.

Well, that is what happened to John. He kept on preaching and baptizing and waiting for his summer to end, but it seemed as if it never would.

In our lesson John said, "After me comes he who is mightier than I." But when? John got tired of his camp-out. He got tired of the crowds. I guess he may even have gotten tired of the strange food.

John had a great sermon to preach, a great mission to complete, but John finally wished his summer would come to an end. Next week John's wilderness ministry will end, and we will see the beginning of the fulfillment of his sermons.

Isn't it nice to think about summer at this time of year, even if it is only for a little while? I love summer!

Third Sunday in Advent

Gospel Lesson: John 1:6-8, 19-28
Key Word: **Fall**
Object: Football

I t is *fall* now. That is our season and our key word for today. If you live in the North it is the time of year when the leaves have turned beautiful colors and some

14

have fallen to the ground. If you are from the West or Southwest the hills will turn green as the rains begin. In the South or Southeast it may just mean it will be getting a little cooler at night.

I have a football here today. This is a sign of fall. Ever since the television set came into our homes the football has become a common sign of fall. A few minutes ago I told you about the different indications that let us know that fall has arrived in the United States and Canada; but no matter where you live football is probably there. On the TV set on Saturday, Sunday, Monday, and Thursday nights, we can view the new national sign of fall—a football.

Remember last week we compared John's ministry in the wilderness to a summer camp? He preached and baptized all who came to his camp. People listened to what he said but they did not understand. Many thought he was the Christ, not just a great prophet.

As John prepared to meet Jesus the fall season of his ministry was approaching. He was challenged by the leader of the temple, "Tell us who you are." John answered once and for all, "I am not the Christ." Many of the people who came to see John had hoped he was the Christ. Now that they knew he was not, John was not as popular as he had been.

If I asked your father to name a football star, then asked your older brother to name one, and then I asked you, all the answers would probably be different.

The football stars shine and then quickly disappear. John was a star. He performed his mission; he introduced Jesus; he preached and baptized. But his mission is not quite complete. We will see him again soon after Christmas when he will baptize Jesus.

John's star will shine once more as his work comes to an end. Fall leads into winter, so next Sunday a whole new season begins.

Fourth Sunday in Advent

Gospel Lesson: Luke 1:26-38
Key Word: **Winter**
Objects: A bathing suit and a glove or another piece of winter clothing

W inter is a funny time of the year. Many who live where it is warm want at least a few days of snow. Some who live where it snows dream about being where it is warm.

I guess that is just the way people are. We always think the other person has the perfect situation, and of course they think we have it perfect.

I was confused about what to use as an object for *winter*, our key word for today. I brought two: one for wherever you may want to go. If you want to be where it is warm, here is our bathing suit left over from summer. If, however, you want to be where it is cold, here is something (name article) for you.

Some people want to go where it is warm so they can swim and enjoy the sun. Others want to go where there is snow so they can ski and have fun in the cold. Older people, such as grandparents, just want it warm so their bodies feel good. They stay in the house where it is warm or go south where they can be in the sunshine.

We know that when Jesus was born in Bethlehem it was winter and pretty cold. It didn't snow in Bethlehem,

16

but it certainly did get cold at night. It was cold that night when Jesus was born. The story told in the lesson today happened in the spring, but the event set in motion ended in the cold of winter. We will celebrate that winter night very soon.

Our Gospel lesson is the beautiful story of the angel coming to Mary to tell her God had chosen her to be the mother of Jesus. Mary was a young girl. Can you imagine what a shock it must have been to be told this?

Two things happened at that time. First Mary believed, and because she believed, it changed her whole life. That is the glory of this Advent season that comes to a close today. It says to us, winter is over. A whole new world is in front of you. If you believe the Advent message—Jesus is coming—your life will be changed forever.

Christmas

(Christmas and Two Sundays after)

T his series entails Christmas Eve or day, depending on when you hold your family service.

The Christmas service is a beautiful, simple, and
dramatic sermon if you prepare for it properly,
according to the instructions. The two Sundays after
Christmas are tied together and deliver a good
post-Christmas message.

Objects Required
☆ candle on a stand
☆ two children
☆ toys

Christmas Eve or Christmas Day

(The Nativity of Our Lord)

Gospel Lesson: Luke 2:1-20
Key Word: **Light**
Object: A candle on a stand

E *xplanation:* To prepare for this sermon you must
have a candle on a rather high stand in the center
aisle so it will be well above the heads of the seated
congregation. If you are having a candle-light service,
don't worry, we will take care of that. You will need
someone to be ready to turn the lights out in the church.
If you usually have the children come forward for the
children's sermon, ask them to go to the back of the
church and stand in the center aisle. (An usher can get
them into an orderly line.) Stand next to the candle and
make the announcement.

This is the Christ candle (unlighted). Tonight it will
show us some amazing things that can change our lives.
(Have someone go to the altar candle and bring a light to
the Christ candle.) Can you all see it? I am a little
disappointed; I thought it would be brighter (turn out all
the lights). Look what happened; the Christ candle
seems to have gotten brighter.

This is just what happened long, long ago in
Bethlehem. The world was too busy to notice what was
happening that cold night. As darkness fell, the light of
the world began to shine from the manger, and suddenly
everyone who wanted to see the light could see.

The Christ candle is so bright I can't see too well. I
think there are some folks in the aisle back there. Would

you please come up here slowly. Oh, now I can see some of you, more of you, now all of you. Gather around so we are in this new light. This Christ candle lights up our whole church.

The light drew the shepherds, the wisemen, then people from all over the world. This one little light turned a dark, hopeless world into a bright world full of hope and joy.

This Christ candle has one more message for all of you. It wants me to tell you to have a very good Christmas, enjoy your gifts, have a good dinner, and enjoy your family. *But* don't forget the light that came to shine on us that night, and let it shine in your hearts all year long.

(If you have a candle-light service, when you turn the lights off there will be a lot of candlelight. Just go ahead, the Christ candle will stand out because you make it special.) Add this ending to today's sermon.

Did you notice all the other candles in the church? These candles represent people all over the world who have heard the message of peace and have accepted the light that came into the world and now shines with the love of the baby Jesus in their lives. You too can be a light to all the world.

First Sunday after Christmas

Gospel Lesson: Luke 2:22-40
Key Word: **Piety**
Objects: Two children

T his a very beautiful Gospel lesson. In it we see two people, a man and a woman, both very old. The man is Simeon, a Pharisee. Most Pharisees were very sincere and pious people. Our word for today is *piety*, which means "devotion to religion and its laws." There was a traditional Jewish piety that was expected of the Pharisees. There were two characteristics of Jewish piety—to observe the law and to always be looking for the Messiah. Simeon observed both of these. He was certainly pious. Anna, the woman in the story, had lived and worked in the Temple most of her life. Simeon and Anna expected the Messiah. When they saw the baby Jesus, he was probably a month old. Simeon and Anna knew right away this baby was the Messiah.

Simeon took the baby and blessed him with words we now call the Nunc Dimittis. God had promised these two old people they would not die until they saw the Messiah. Simeon said these words as he held the baby, "Lord, now lettest thy servant depart in peace. . . ." He was ready to die; God's promise was fulfilled.

Are there two children here today who have wanted something for Christmas so very much that maybe you said, If I don't get that I will just die? Did anyone want something that bad? Did you get it for Christmas? Two of you come up here, but first, whatever it is you wanted must be small enough so that next week you can bring it to church. All right. We have two children. Do not tell us what you wanted. Did you really wish and wish for this gift? Did you get very excited when you saw it? All right, you bring it next Sunday so we can see what you were dying to get.

Simeon and Anna wanted something very much before they died, and God gave them their gift. It was not a gift just for Simeon and Anna, it was a gift for all of us—the best gift God had to give, the best gift we will ever receive.

Do not forget your gifts next week. We will be waiting to see what you received.

Second Sunday after Christmas

Gospel Lesson: John 1:1-18
Word: **Flesh**
Objects: The two children from last week with toys

D o you remember last week we talked about Simeon and Anna, who saw the baby Jesus in the Temple and knew he was the Messiah? Remember that God had told them they would not die until they had seen Jesus? Their greatest wish was fulfilled. We talked about how we sometimes wish for something and if we do not get it we feel as if we will just die. There were two children here who told us they felt the same way about something they wanted, but they were lucky enough to get their wish and they did not die. They are here today to show us their gifts.

Come up and let us see your gifts. Oh, they are great gifts! Tell me the truth; if you had not gotten these gifts would you really have died? I think not. Let us play a little game. How many of you can remember what you wanted last Christmas? Some of you may be able to, and that is fine. Sometimes when I want something very much I forget what it is before I get it. So often we want the special toy of the year that is advertised on television, and when we get it, it is not as great as the television made it seem. The TV picture and the toy turned to flesh are two different things. Last week Simeon and Anna waited so long, and when they saw Jesus in the flesh they were not disappointed. Our key word today is *flesh*. We know what that means; we are in the flesh right here.

In the Gospel today it is a long time later, about thirty years. John the Baptist is preaching to all who will listen about the Messiah who is now among them in the flesh. It is John who will introduce Jesus to us. That was why John came, and he will complete his mission.

A few minutes ago I asked you what it was you wanted so much for Christmas last year. Some of you could remember and some could not. Suppose I asked you a harder question now. What did Simeon and Anna and John the Baptist and you and I get for Christmas, not last year or ten years ago but two thousand years ago? I cannot remember what I received last year, but I can remember the gift God gave us all two thousand years ago. The Word—that is God; the flesh—that is Jesus. The gift of two thousand years ago is remembered even today. Don't ever forget it.

Epiphany

(Series One—Four Sundays)

T his series of lessons is presented during the Epiphany season. The Epiphany is a prime Christian feast commemorating three events: the baptism of Jesus (Mark 1); the visit of the three wise men to Bethlehem (Matthew 2); and the miracle Jesus performed at the wedding in Cana (John 2).

The feast is celebrated on January 6 and is also called the Twelfth Day; its eve is called the Twelfth Night.

The first four Sundays of this series have stories dealing with lines and what a few lines can do in telling a story. The items below will be used for drawings that will add interest in the stories for the first four weeks. The drawings will be very simple; you will have no trouble with them. If you feel uncomfortable as the artist, enlist someone else. But you can do it, trust me.

Objects Required
☆ artist's pad or poster board
☆ easel
☆ felt pen (black)

The Baptism of Our Lord

(First Sunday after the Epiphany)

Gospel Lesson: Mark 1:4-11
Key Word: **Came**
Object: Two lines drawn on artist's pad

T he next four Sundays we will be making a picture. We will add a few lines each week, and in the end you will be surprised what a story a few lines can tell.

This Sunday is called the Baptism of Our Lord. That is a very important place for us to start. Baptism is the beginning of your Christian commitment.

Jesus came from Galilee to be baptized by John in the River Jordan. He did not ride in a taxi or borrow a car to take him to the Jordan; he walked. Only the very rich had ox carts or chariots to ride in; others walked.

Now we come to the first two lines of our picture. Remember, a few lines can tell a story. Are you ready? (If there is an older child who can draw, it would be great to enlist his help as your resident line maker for the next few weeks.)

Our word for today is *came*. Jesus came to John. That is a clue to what this drawing is supposed to be. It looks as if it could be a tree, or maybe a sliding board. Can anyone guess what it is? If you can't guess I will have to tell you, but first I want you to know my feelings may be hurt if my art is so bad you cannot guess what this is. All right, it is a road. Back to our key word. Jesus came to John. He came down this road to the River Jordan from Galilee. (Point from top to bottom of the drawing.)

Jesus came to be baptized. Do you remember that before Christmas we said John the Baptist would be back? Here he is again, John the Baptizer. Now the name fits him as it never did before. This is the time to baptize Jesus. John came with a mission—to announce that Jesus was coming and to baptize him so that the ministry of Jesus could begin.

John was the first to announce the start of Jesus' ministry of preaching and teaching love and forgiveness. We know John did his job well because after he baptized Jesus a voice from heaven said, "Thou art my beloved Son; with thee I am well pleased."

Jesus is off down the road to meet us.

Second Sunday after the Epiphany

Gospel Lesson: John 1:35-42
Key Word: **Follow**
Object: Another line on the drawing

H ere we are back again with our two lines from last week. Who can tell me what these lines are? That is right, a road. Last week Jesus came down this road to be baptized by John the Baptizer and to start his ministry.

You remember we talked about John the Baptist and his camp in the wilderness next to the River Jordan?

John had a few disciples who stayed with him during his time out in the wilds.

Who can tell me what a disciple is? The dictionary defines it pretty well—a follower of Jesus, especially one of the twelve apostles.

John the Baptist leads his disciples to Jesus with this last witness, "Behold the Lamb of God." These two men, John and Andrew, were the first followers of Jesus.

This Sunday Jesus is not going to come down the road the way he did last week. Today he will go back up the road and begin to preach the message of love and forgiveness. As Jesus went up the road there were many kinds of people who came out to meet him. We know that when Jesus looks at us he does not see what others see. He looks right through us and sees what is in our hearts. That is what happened on the walk up the road. People came out to meet Jesus. He looked straight into their hearts and said, "*Follow* me," and they did. And that is our word for today.

Jesus was walking and his disciples were following him. These disciples were like you and me. Sometimes when we try to follow Jesus, we are a little afraid of where he is leading us. The disciples started to get tired so they said to Jesus, "Where are you staying?" He said, "Come and see."

Here we are back on our road. It is not a very fancy road and it has one big problem. It doesn't go anywhere. Just as the disciples left everything to follow Jesus, then wondered where they were going, that is our problem.

Our road does not lead anywhere. A road should lead somewhere, so let us put one more line on our picture and make the road stop somewhere and go somewhere.

(Draw one line at the top of the road.)

Look what happened. The road seems to stop here at the horizon. A horizon is that place where the earth and the sky seem to meet. Jesus and his disciples went up the road toward the horizon to start a trip filled with high and low spots, with miracles and harsh words, with victories and defeats.

What is over the horizon for them and for us is always a mystery. Next Sunday we'll add a few more lines and see more of Jesus' journey with his disciples.

Third Sunday after the Epiphany

Gospel Lesson: Mark 1:14-20
Key Word: **Immediately**
Object: Boat

L et us start today by looking at our picture. It is slowly starting to take shape. Remember we began with these two lines (point to lines) that made a road. Then we added this line we called the horizon (point). Today we are going to see something on the horizon and we will see where we are going.

Remember in the Gospel lesson Jesus went to the Sea of Galilee? At the sea he saw a boat. Let us add a boat.

Our road took Jesus and his first disciples up to the horizon. On the horizon they found the Sea of Galilee. There on the sea was a boat with fishermen and their nets.

A strange thing happened. Jesus said to them, "Follow me." *Follow* was our key word from last week. John had two faithful followers and he told them to follow Jesus. Here Jesus is telling two other fishermen he met to follow him. *Immediately*, and that is our word for today, the men left their nets and followed him.

This is something I had not counted on, had you? The two fishermen, Simon and Andrew, took one look at Jesus and after he said "follow me" they left everything they had and loved and followed him. That is very hard to believe. Do you think Jesus expects us to get up and leave grandparents and family and follow him? I hope not. I do not think I am ready to have my children leave everything and follow someone.

What Jesus is really doing here is starting the very first church. He will pick twelve men and say to them that they are the first church. If there are to be more churches in the future it is up to them. They will have the word that will make the difference.

We are part of that great church and just like its members. All the men Jesus picked were not strong in the faith. Some fell by the way as Judas did, some doubted as Thomas, some denied like Peter. But with all their human weaknesses they built the church we have today.

You children are disciples. You will have to pick the right thing to do and not follow the crowd if what they are doing is wrong. Follow Jesus' way. You are his disciples. You are members of his church. Some of you may be strong, some weak, but there is room for all in our church. You do not have to leave your family to be a disciple. When Jesus says to do it his way, you can do it.

Fourth Sunday after the Epiphany

Gospel Lesson: Mark 1:21-28
Key Word: **Taught**
Object: Drawing of a church

Today we will finish our picture. We had the road, the horizon, the boat, and now the last and most important part of our picture. If you listened to the Gospel lesson, you may know what the last thing is we need. A church.

Our picture is finished. That is really some artwork. Let us see what happens in this church. This is the synagogue at Capernaum. A synagogue is a Jewish church and has no cross, so our church is without a cross also. Jesus picked this place to start teaching because it was a crossroads town. Not a big city but one that had all kinds of people—Greeks, Jews, Romans, business people, fishermen, and rich people. Jesus picked this spot to establish himself as a teacher. He did his first teaching in a strange but really effective way.

He taught as if he knew God. Not just from the Old Testament scriptures, but things they had never heard. He talked about God as if he were a friend and he knew him in a personal way. The people in the synagogue where he taught were impressed with him and his teachings.

In those days there were people who were thought to be strange and possessed. No one understood them. Today we know these people may have some mental illness or epilepsy, but in Jesus' day these were said to be "possessed by demons." It was believed there were little demons flying all around looking for a body to get into and take it over. The priests did many strange things to make these demons come out, but they never succeeded. Jesus *taught*, that's our key word this week. This is the beginning of Jesus' teaching ministry that never ended.

Jesus taught as "one who had authority," and they were astonished. Now we see what Jesus' teaching was like. It had authority. Do you know anyone in your life who speaks with authority? Your mom, your dad, your teacher, even I have some authority. Authority means "the power to enforce obedience." That was the new kind of teaching Jesus brought to God's word that day. The power to back up words with deeds.

When Jesus saw this man who was possessed he said, "Come out," and the demon came out. What really happened was that the man was healed; he was no longer sick. Jesus did not use only words, he used deeds, and his fame spread all through Galilee.

Now it is our turn to be teachers. I do not care what size you are, big or little; what age you are, young or old;

you can be a teacher if you want to. You can be a teacher like the scribes and Pharisees who just used words, or you can be a teacher like Jesus and use words and deeds. It is easy to say "be good." It is much harder to say "be good so that others know you are good." Words and deeds—that is real teaching and living.

Epiphany

(*Series Two—Five Sundays*)

These next four Sundays we will talk about miracles of healing and other miracles. We will look at the miracles Jesus performed and then try to help the children understand that a miracle is anything that seems impossible. Very simple objects will be used to illustrate that the commonplace things of today were miracles only yesterday.

The last Sunday, the Transfiguration of our Lord, we will use the pastor as the object, and he will be transformed before their eyes.

Objects Required

☆ flashlight
☆ bottle of children's aspirin
☆ book of matches
☆ bandage
☆ light bulb
☆ bottle of something for upset stomach
☆ piece of new cloth
☆ old shirt
☆ pastor

Fifth Sunday after the Epiphany

Gospel Lesson: Mark 1:29-39
Key Word: **Sick**
Objects: Flashlight, bottle of children's aspirin

T he last half of the Epiphany season commemorates the time when all the sick people found
Jesus. *Sick* is our word for today; we all know what that
means. Last week we had a man possessed by a demon.
Today Jesus is still in Capernaum. Knowing that Simon
lives nearby, he decides to spend the night there, in
Simon's mother-in-law's house. He went from the
temple to her house expecting to have a good dinner and
a nice rest. When Jesus arrived at the house, Simon's
mother-in-law was sick; she had a fever. Jesus went into
her room, took her hand, and the fever left. She was well
enough to serve dinner, and by the time they had eaten,
a crowd had gathered around the house. Some of these
people had every disease imaginable. Jesus healed them
all. The next morning he went out to a lonely place to
pray. They had a long journey ahead of them and he was
tired. He told his disciples, "Let us move on; we have a
lot of preaching to do, throughout Galilee." You boys
and girls know there are no miracles today. Or are
there? Just imagine what those people two thousand
years ago would have thought if you had walked around
with this flashlight. (Hold it up.) We use flashlights all
the time. You push the button and just like that a beam
of light shines, taking away the darkness. This flashlight
would have been a miracle years ago. In fact even
George Washington would have thought that a flashlight was a miracle.

We are talking about miracles and also about healing.

34

Here is another miracle, a bottle of aspirins. When you are in pain, your mother will give you an aspirin and you will feel better. Not a big miracle; we can even explain how aspirin works on your body to relieve the pain. What we accept as ordinary today were considered miracles in the past. They help us to understand the miracles that Jesus did in healing the sick so long ago.

Sixth Sunday after the Epiphany

Gospel Lesson: Mark 1:40-45
Key Word: **Pity**
Objects: A match and a bandage

J esus is still finding sick people wherever he goes. Today he is going to do some big healing. Leprosy was one of the most dreaded diseases you could have. We do not have to go into how horrible a disease it was. But if you had leprosy you were not allowed to live near other people. You were sent away to die all alone. You must admit this does not seem very nice, and Jesus found this to be a real challenge. One leper man said, "If you will, you can make me clean." Jesus had pity on this man. And that is our word for today, *pity*. Pity means "to feel sorry for someone who is suffering or otherwise unhappy." Jesus looked at the man and said, "I will; be clean." And the man was clean; his leprosy was gone. A really big miracle.

Today I have a miracle that would have blown the minds of people in Jesus' day. Look at this. Do you know what it is? A book of matches (hold up). In Bible times a flint was used to start the oil lamps to burning, but most of the time one was left burning as a kind of permanent match. Can you imagine the surprise if you showed up with a match and said, May I give you a light? That would have been called a miracle. In Jesus' day, if you had a sore, infection was a big problem. Today if we are hurt or wounded we pull out one of our modern miracles, a bandage (hold up). It is put on our sore, and in a few days, since it keeps the dirt out, the sore will be healed—another miracle we don't even think about.

Little miracles help us to understand big miracles. Jesus showed pity for the man in trouble. We can learn to show pity to those in need also.

Seventh Sunday after the Epiphany

Gospel Lesson: Mark 2:1-12
Key Word: **Forgiven**
Objects: A light bulb, a bottle of something for upset stomach

J esus had just returned from another preaching trip. He was tired and ready for some home-cooked food and a little rest. The people of the area had heard about the miracles he had performed on his trip, and they were waiting for him when he returned to Capernaum. The sick had been brought by their friends, hoping to be healed. They crowded into the house and courtyard. Four men who had brought one of their sick friends on a stretcher could not get to the door because of the crowd. So they climbed onto the roof, made an opening, and lowered their friend down to Jesus. They certainly did get his attention! Jesus looked at the man, then at the scribes who were there. The scribes were in charge of being certain the Jewish laws were being kept. They always watched Jesus. The law said, "Great prophets can heal people but only God can forgive a sin." As usual, Jesus used this as a chance to teach. He said to the man, "Your sins are forgiven." *Forgiven* is our word for today. Well, this was more than the scribes could handle. Jesus knew what they were thinking—another lesson for the scribes. "Why do you question in your hearts?" Jesus said. That must have scared the scribes—how could this man be a mind and heart reader? Then Jesus said, "Which is easier to say to the paralytic, 'Your sins are forgiven,' or 'Rise, take up your pallet and walk'?" All the miracles end the same for those who are looking for the miracle, "We never saw anything like this."

We have been talking about the things we take for granted today that would have been thought of as miracles in Jesus' time. Today I have two. They have one thing in common: they are both packaged in glass. Ready? A light bulb (hold it up). Imagine, if the people would have thought the flashlight we had last week was a miracle, what they would think about a light bulb.

This is a glass bottle that has something for an upset stomach in it. When you tell your mother your stomach hurts she gives you a little bit of this, and in a few minutes your stomachache starts to feel better. What a miracle this would have been in those days.

Earlier in this sermon I said that Jesus never stops teaching and never misses a chance to help us understand. Jesus can heal us and forgive our sin, one at a time or both at once. That is the message of our miracle today, "Go, your sins are forgiven."

Eighth Sunday after the Epiphany

Gospel Lesson: Mark 2:18-22
Key Word: **New**
Objects: A piece of new cloth, an old shirt

I n our Gospel lesson for today Jesus is facing a new and different challenge—this time from the Pharisees. All good Jews fasted on the Sabbath and high holy days. Jesus' disciples were not too faithful to the old laws. So the scribes and the Pharisees were always ready to say, "Bad, bad, you just broke the law." When they questioned Jesus about this he answered right away, "Can the wedding guests fast while the bridegroom is with them?" Then to teach the lesson so all could understand he used two stories that were very simple.

I have here a piece of cloth (hold it up). It is sanforized, that means it is "preshrunk," it is *new*, our word for today. If I tore my shirt and wanted to patch it, I could use this piece of material and sew it over the hole. My shirt is old, has been washed many times, and will not shrink anymore. This material has been treated with chemicals so that it won't shrink either. You should always try to buy clothes that will not shrink, because if you do not they will not fit when you wash them. In Jesus' day most clothes were made of wool or linen. Both of these materials can shrink. Sanforized cloth would have been the miracle. Jesus told the people, "No one sews a piece of unshrunk cloth on an old garment; if he does, the patch tears away from it, the new from the old, and a worse tear is made."

Wineskins get brittle when they get old. If you put in new wine, as it ferments it may expand and burst the old skins; then you lose the wine and the wineskin.

I am talking about a new way of life—that is our word, *new*. Jesus told the Pharisees, "Listen to me, I have a new way of life. I have a new gospel. Do not keep patching up the old laws. Let me show you the new way."

I think he may be talking to us today. Follow the new way.

The Transfiguration of Our Lord

(Last Sunday after the Epiphany)

Gospel Lesson: Mark 9:2-9
Key Word: **Transfigured**
Object: The Pastor

Our Gospel lesson for today is one that is full of hidden lessons. I think you children can understand these lessons as well as your parents. This will not be an easy sermon to follow, so you must pay close attention.

First we start with, "After six days." Whenever God had something big to show to people he always sent them up on a mountain. They had to wait and pray for six days, and on the seventh day a revelation would come. Today it is pretty much the same. Your folks say you will go to the big amusement park next week or you will get a bike for your birthday. We always have to wait for the big things to happen. Moses had to wait up on a mountain for six days so that he could receive the Ten Commandments.

Peter, James, and John were with Jesus on the

mountain. Six days passed and Jesus was *transfigured*—that means "changed"—right before their eyes. His clothes became a glowing white. He was changed.

Now I am going to be transfigured right before your eyes. You did not know I could do that, did you? I won't have to go to a mountaintop or wait six days; I can do it right now in front of you. Are you ready? Count for me 1, 2, 3. Okay—1, 2, 3 . . . (walk out of the altar area and sit in a pew). I am a layperson sitting in the pew. I am not the minister right now, I am one of you. I am transfigured. While I am sitting here transfigured let me tell you the second big message of this lesson. Moses and Elijah were Old Testament prophets. They lived by the law, the old law. If people did not respond to God's message or got in the way of his people they were killed. All the stories of Moses and Elijah are full of people dying for not listening to God. Moses and Elijah disappeared, and Jesus was left standing alone with his message of love not death, of forgiveness not condemnation. The old law has passed away and the new one has taken its place.

The message of the Gospel is now love and forgiveness. To make certain there was no confusion a voice came from heaven that said, "This is my beloved Son; listen to him." Peter, James, and John knew Jesus as few other men knew him. You can know him in the same way.

I am going to be transfigured again or the service will not continue. Give me a 1, 2, 3, so I can be your pastor again. Ready? 1, 2, 3.

Lent

(Five Sundays and Palm Sunday)

I n this series we will be talking about moving ahead in life, things we can change and things we cannot. Life is filled with mistakes and the correction of these mistakes. We also have many times when we would like to be able to change something but it is impossible to do so.

The lessons will give us a chance to watch Jesus grow during this Lenten season and show the children how we must accept our actions as final. We do not always have the luxury of changing.

Objects Required

☆ pencil with an eraser, ball point pen, pad or paper
☆ sign—a bad word
☆ paper plate, plastic plate
☆ sign—one side, LOVE; other side, HATE
☆ golf club or tennis racquet (symbol of your favorite pastime)
☆ palm branch or palm frond

First Sunday in Lent

Gospel Lesson: Mark 1:9-15
Key Word: **Dove**
Objects: Pencil, eraser, pen, paper

This is the time when Jesus became a man. He came down from the little town of Galilee, where he had spent his life, to be baptized. Then he was sent into the desert to be tempted.

In the days when Jesus was growing up people thought that the devil lived out in the desert. They thought that all the wild beasts were under the control of the devil. Jesus went into the land of the devil with all those wild animals to harm and scare him. No wonder I said this is the time Jesus became a man. This was done so that Jesus would be able to pass the tests that all the great prophets of old had to pass. Moses and Elijah had to spend time in the desert, and God wanted to show that his Son was no different and did not get special treatment. He had to prove he was ready; no mistake, he was ready to go forward and never turn back.

There are many times in our lives when we must make decisions to go forward and not look back. I have asked two children to come up to show us times in our lives when we reach that kind of decision. Some of you may think that it is not such a big time, but let me tell you it is.

I have here a big pad. I want you to take your pencil and write my name on the pad, nice and big so everyone can see it. Do you know how to spell my name? All right. I will help you. My name is Smith, *S-m-u-t-h*. Smith. Oh my goodness, I made a mistake. I spelled my name wrong. It isn't spelled with a *u*, it is spelled *S-m-i-t-h*.

Erase that *u* and make it an *i*, please. Now that is a lot better. Now my name is spelled right. It sure was a lucky thing we could change the spelling and correct our mistake.

Now, will you come up and bring your pen? I would like you to write what happened to Jesus in the desert. Write the word *tempted*. If you can't spell it, I will help you. Can you spell the word *tempted*? All right, *t-e-m-p-t-e-d*. Let us check to be sure; remember I did not do too well with my own name. Yes, it is spelled right, and it's a good thing it is because this is in ink and you cannot just erase it to change it. We start with a pencil with an eraser when we are not too sure, but as we become more certain of ourselves we switch to a pen because we don't expect to make mistakes.

As we grow up we turn our backs on the past and head into the future. How do we know when we are ready to move up? One day our teacher will say, I want you to bring in a pen tomorrow; we will be using that instead of a pencil.

When Jesus was ready God sent a dove. That was God's sign of peace and love to his Son. It was a message Jesus was to preach as long as he lived. Our word today is *dove*, the sign God sent to tell his Son it was time to preach the new gospel of peace and love.

During Lent we will talk about moving ahead and things we can change and things we cannot change.

Second Sunday in Lent

Gospel Lesson: Mark 8:31-38
Key Word: **Rebuke**
Object: A bad word

I n our lesson today Jesus got angry. He told Peter off in no uncertain terms. He said, "Get behind me Satan! For you are not on the side of God, but of men."

If your mom or dad said something similar to that to you, I guess you would go to your room and stay out of sight until you were certain they were in a better mood. In the stories in the Bible about Jesus he does not get angry very often. When he does it is usually at strangers like the scribes and Pharisees.

Do you know why he got so mad at Peter? You remember when Satan took Jesus out in the desert and he tempted Jesus by offering him the whole world if Jesus would bow down to him? Then it would not be necessary for Jesus to die. Now Peter is telling Jesus, "You don't have to die." Jesus said to Peter, "You are just like Satan. I must die. Get away from me."

This Lenten season we are talking about things we can change and things we cannot change. A bad word for instance. It says Peter began to rebuke Jesus. That is our word, *rebuke*. Does anyone know what it means? It means "to criticize sharply or to scold." No wonder Jesus did not like what Peter said. If you tried to scold your folks I think they would get upset.

You can never take a bad word back. You can say, I am sorry I said it, or you can say, I love you. All that helps the person you hurt, but there is no way to ever get that word back. That is why we have to be so careful when we get angry at the people we love. They do things to enrage or make us angry sometimes, but hold your tongue.

After Jesus was no longer angry at Peter's bad words he tried to explain just why he got mad. This all started when Jesus said, "I must be rejected and killed." This upset Peter. Jesus now explains what he meant. If you have a job to do and it is dangerous, you might even die doing that job. So you don't do your job and you save your life. What good is your life if you have failed? If your life is not worth giving, your life is not worth living. Jesus said to Peter that day, and he says it to us every day of our lives. "I died so you could live. Your life was worth my dying to save you."

Don't be bad. Don't get angry. Don't say words you would like to take back. Love one another even as I have loved you. Then you will live a life worth dying for.

Third Sunday in Lent

Gospel Lesson: John 2:13-22
Key Word: **Cheat**
Objects: Paper plate, plastic plate

L ast week I told you Jesus did not often get mad or angry. When he did it was usually with strangers not friends. Today he was angry; so angry he struck at people. The lesson says he made a whip of cords. You all know what a whip is. Let us try to find out why he was so angry. Jesus did not make a whip and strike out at people because he hated them. He did it because they were breaking God's law and showing disrespect for God's house, the Temple.

The people who upset Jesus were ordinary people. They sold sheep or oxen or pigeons. Some were money changers. The people had little stands set up on the grounds of the Temple. They rented the space from the priests, and they cut the Temple in on some of the profits.

There were money changers, because when you came to the Temple for services on high holy days a tax had to be paid. The people who came to Passover had only Roman money, and the tax was to be paid in Jewish half shekels. The money changers charged a fee to have the money changed so they made a profit. That was what made Jesus angry. These money changers would *cheat* the poor people, and the priests knew about it and did not stop it. That is our word for today.

At Passover a sacrifice was brought to the altar. It was to be alive and the best you had to offer. People would travel for a week to get to the Temple, and they could not bring their animals for sacrifice. It was such a long trip. Animals could be bought in the courtyard of the temple if that was what you wanted to offer. The people who sold these animals cheated the people. They did not have the best for sale. They had skinny old animals and pigeons. This sacrifice was to be the best you had to offer God; instead it was a racket, performed right in the Temple.

Jesus was very angry when he saw what was happening. He took that whip and drove the people right out of the Temple. They knew they had broken the law, so they got up and ran away without a fight.

Jesus changed the Temple and the lives of the people who came to worship that Passover. He was not angry because the animals were being sold or money was being changed, he was mad because this was being done in the Temple and people who had no choice but to do business with the money changers were being cheated.

I need two children to help me with a demonstration. (One child will get a paper plate; the other a plastic plate.) Hold up these plates and I am going to draw three sections on one (paper) and four on the other (plastic). Now, what if you were selling plate lunches or dinners, and you had three items of food on the paper plates and four on the plastic plates? Those to whom you sold the paper plates would be cheated, right? Because the plastic plates would have more food, and the paper plates just might get too soggy and those buying the paper plates might lose all of their food. You would not want to cheat the people. Therefore, you'd have to make them all the same.

God is ready to change us and forgive us no matter what happens. Some things we can change and some we cannot. Do not give up, keep trying.

Fourth Sunday in Lent

Gospel Lesson: John 3:14-21
Key Word: **Famous**
Object: Sign: LOVE on one side; HATE on the other

T his children's sermon is a bit different from most of our sermons. First, our word is not in the Gospel lesson. Second, we are going to talk about four-letter words; and as you know they are usually "bad" words, which we would not use in church.

Our word for today is *famous*. Movie stars are

famous, the president of the United States is famous. In this church even I am famous. All that means is the person is very well known. What do you think the word *famous* has to do with our Gospel lesson for today? Can anyone guess?

One verse in the lesson is the most famous in the whole Bible, John 3:16: "For God so loved the world that he gave his only Son, that whoever believes in him should not perish but have eternal life." That verse is so famous that even people who do not believe in God know it. Many people say that this verse is the whole Bible in one verse. Most of you know it; that includes the adults here today too. Let's say it together: "For God so loved the world that he gave his only Son, that whoever believes in him should not perish but have eternal life."

For the past few weeks we have been talking about things we can change and things we cannot change. Now we are going to talk about four-letter words. I know these can be changed. I would like to ask you for some four-letter words, but I am a little afraid to do that. I'll start with a four-letter word and say it right here in church. If you think you should hold your ears, do so, but here goes my four-letter word. I will say it softly the first time so that I won't shock you. Ready—Love! Did you all hear that four-letter word? Love. That is one of the key words in our Gospel today. "God loved." God loved you so much he gave his Son to die so you and you and you can live forever.

(Hold up sign—LOVE.) There it is, love. Now that I've said a four-letter word in church I will try a bad four-letter word. Here we go—HATE. (Turn the sign over to show HATE.) Do you see the choice we have here today? Love, hate, it is just that easy.

48

If you want to hate, you look real hard and you can find something to hate. If you want to love you can find something to love. That is what the last part of the Gospel says. If you want to hate me, look on my dark side. If you want to love me, look on my bright side.

This has been a big day for you. First you met a famous man—at least here in this church I am famous. Then you learned the most famous verse in the Bible, and to top it all off, you learned a four-letter word you can say in church.

I love you all even as God loves you all. He taught me how to love; that is why I can love you.

Fifth Sunday in Lent

Gospel Lesson: John 12:20-33
Key Word: **Life**
Object: Object representing pastor's favorite pastime—for example, golf club, tennis racquet, book

I have here a (golf club, tennis racquet, whatever). Are you thinking, What does that have to do with the Gospel for today? Let me tell you about this _____ and the trouble I have because I love to _____. Sometimes when I have to make calls or write a sermon or visit the sick, I think, This is a perfect day for me to _____. I just love it, it relaxes me, and I know it is good for me to get away from the pressures of the church once in a while. Many times I would like to give up everything else and just _____.

If you were here last week when we talked about love and hate you will remember four-letter words. They are back again this week, but it is a little strange. Jesus says if you love life you lose it, if you hate life you keep it. That is pretty deep for kids; let me see if I can explain this so you can understand a little better.

When you get a new toy and you decide it is your favorite, you know right away that someday that toy will be lost or broken. It just seems to happen. You still love it best of all. When you get a new puppy or kitten you love that pet so much. You know that someday it may get lost or die but you still love it. You also love your friends and family, but you know they may move away or die, but you love them.

Jesus loved his life. But when Satan said, "You don't have to die," Jesus said he would do what he had to do to save the world.

Just as you love that toy or pet, your friends and family, you should never love anything so much that you would give anything in the world to save it. That is what Jesus is saying about loving life and losing it. Jesus would not make a deal to save his life. He loved life just as we do, but he loved us more.

There have been many stories in the news about people who were real heroes. (If at all possible try to relate a tale of recent heroism.) Another person was in danger of losing his life and this stranger rushed in and, at a great personal risk, saved that person. Sure that person loved his own life, but he didn't love it so much that he forgot the rest of the people around him.

You don't have to hate your life to keep it, just do not love it too much.

On one of the beautiful spring days that we will soon be having I know I will pick up my _____ and be tempted to just forget the rest of the world and go out and do my thing, but I know I will say to myself, *Do not love it too much or you will lose it.*

I am sure this kind of balance in your life is not easy. Not for you or your folks or your pastor. (Swing the club or racquet and walk away.)

Palm Sunday

(Sunday of the Passion)

Gospel Lesson: Mark 11:1-11
Key Word: **Hosanna**
Object: Palm branch or frond

E veryone likes a parade. I know I do, and when I go to a parade there are always lots of people; so I know you all like parades.

Today, Palm Sunday, we are celebrating a very famous parade. This parade changed the whole world. Most parades do not change anything. When they are over we say, I had a good time, and then it is forgotten.

This Palm Sunday parade did not end. It started a whole new way to live. It introduced a new King to the world. He became the most famous King in history. This was the King of kings and Lord of lords. Now, that is what I call a parade!

Something else happened on that day that may sound a little strange. Remember in the Gospel lesson the people waved palm branches and shouted "Hosanna"? I do not know about you, but that word *hosanna* is strange to me. How many of you have used that word this week? I said many hellos and goodbyes, but never did I say *hosanna*. Not once.

Does anybody know what hosanna means? That is our word for today and I was hoping someone would know what it means. How about the grown-ups? Any help from you?

I will tell you so that the next time we hear it we will know what it means. It is from a Hebrew word that means "save." The people who watched the parade on

Palm Sunday were waiting and looking for a king to save them. As Jesus rode through the town they hoped he was the king who would save them so they called out, Hosanna.

This parade did not just go down the main street because it was a nice wide street to use for a parade. The Jewish people thought that when the Messiah came he would appear on the Mount of Olives and ride in triumph to the Temple. That is exactly what Jesus did that day.

All of you have a big palm branch. (If you do not distribute palms, have branches cut from green paper.) Why don't we show the whole world that we want Jesus to save us too. All of you stand and wave the branches and call out Hosanna, just the way they did so long ago. We will say, "Hosanna, save us, Hosanna, save us."

We need it and we believe Jesus can do it today.

Easter

(Seven Sundays)

T he children's sermon for Easter Day is a short one since the service is usually long. The six Sundays following Easter are a bit different in that we have a key word but no objects are listed that you supply. The children will bring objects in for this series.

It is important that you convey your discomfort at not having control of the objects, but at the same time show your confidence in the children doing their jobs well.

In order to prepare for the second Sunday of Easter, you will need to ask a child to bring something he would want to have with him if he were going to be alone for a while. This should be done at some time during the week before that Sunday.

If children need some help deciding what to bring, a flashlight, a good book, a teddy bear, food, sweater, or blanket could be some suggestions. If a child forgets his object one Sunday, simply walk to a pew or the altar and pick up a Bible and say, We can always use this.

Objects Required
☆ raw egg
☆ suitcase, old looking if possible

Easter Day

(The Resurrection of Our Lord)

Gospel Lesson: Mark 16:1-8
Key Word: **Risen**
Object: An uncooked egg

H appy Easter! The service on Easter Day is always longer than on other Sundays, so the children's sermon will be shorter.

I do want to make two points today. Our word is *risen*. Let me tell you what the dictionary says about risen—"the past tense of rise."

In our Gospel for today the angel said to the two Marys, "He is risen." He rose from death to life before we knew it. It is past tense. That means it already happened. That is the message I have for you and for everyone. It already happened. He is risen.

He was dead, now he lives forever. When you rise you must do it on your own. Someone can help you to stand up, but that is not rising. That is being helped to stand. If you rise you do it all by yourself. Jesus rose. He did it.

Here is an egg. This egg has many similarities to Jesus in the tomb. Inside is a little chicken. He is trapped in the egg. If he wants to rise and grow, he must get out of this shell. No one will help him; he has to do it on his own. He will peck at the hard shell until he finally breaks through.

You do not have to be like the little chick in this egg. You do not have to be like Jesus, trapped in the tomb. He is risen. He set us free. He is with us every minute of every day.

We do not have to always do it on our own. We can call on Jesus and say, Help me.

Happy Easter! We are not alone.

Second Sunday of Easter

Gospel Lesson: John 20:19-31
Key Word: **Fear**
Object: ?

This is the second Sunday of Easter. Last week was Easter Day and that was the first Sunday of Easter. Today we will start a new series of children's sermons. Each Sunday we have a key word and an object to help teach us a lesson. For the next six Sundays I have key words; they were no problem, but the objects were.

I have my suitcase with me just as if I were going on a trip. I am not going anywhere, but Jesus is going to go away.

The reason I do not have any objects for these weeks is because I want you children to supply them. Does it seem strange to have an object lesson without any objects?

In the Gospel lesson for today we find the disciples with the doors shut and locked because they were afraid Jesus was dead. He was crucified on Good Friday; some people said he rose again on Easter Day. The disciples were not too sure so they thought the safest thing to do was to hide, just in case the priests were looking for them. These men were afraid. Our word today is *fear;* that means "being afraid of something known or unknown." These men were not even certain of whom or what they were afraid. Jesus appeared to them suddenly. They must have jumped in fright. "Peace be with you," was the first thing he said to them. I am sure they felt much better now that they knew Jesus was alive; just as he said he would be. No old tomb could hold him. They were no longer afraid.

Isn't it funny how sometimes when we are afraid something happens, and we no longer have any fear? Perhaps you have been alone in your house and you heard strange sounds. You did not know what they were and you were afraid; then your mother returned and your fear went away.

Jesus is going away soon. I have a suitcase here and I must tell you a secret. I asked one of you earlier this week to bring something small that would fit in my suitcase. Something you would want to have with you if you were left alone for a while. I am going to be surprised when _____ brings up the special item _____ has chosen. Oh, look what we have here. Would you tell us why you chose this to have with you if you were left alone for a while? Good. Thank you, now we will put it into our suitcase to start our collection of important things. This week Jesus left the Holy Spirit with his disciples to give them peace and to take away their fear.

Will someone bring something in next week that will fit into the suitcase? Fine. You bring an object for next week. Maybe your parents can help you remember.

Third Sunday of Easter

Gospel Lesson: Luke 24:35-48
Key Word: **Witnesses**
Object: ?

O ur first object lesson sermon went rather well last week, considering I did not have an object. I hope we do just as well today. Our word this week is *witnesses*. People who have seen something with their own eyes and can tell what they saw are witnesses. This word is at the end of the Gospel; often it is at the beginning. The reason it is at the end is to show you the most important thing the lesson has to teach us. Jesus lived with his disciples for three years. During the time they were together Jesus told them time and again, "I will go away, then in three days I will return." This is exactly what happened. Now Jesus is back and his disciples are still not certain they believe what is happening. They keep wanting to see one more sign of proof that this is really Jesus and not someone else. Just one more sign.

Jesus shows them several things—his hands and feet, then he takes a piece of fish and eats it to show he is not a ghost. At last he looks at us, you and me, right from this lesson, and says "You and you and you (point to the children), are witnesses to these things."

If you believe in Jesus then you are a witness. You have to get up on the witness stand every time you have a chance with your friends and say, "I believe. I am a witness."

Jesus is still telling his friends he is going away. Remember I have no object for this lesson. Someone is bringing in an object that they would like to have with them if they are going to be alone for a long time. Who has our object? Ah, there you are. Before we see what is important to _____, remember this may not be important to the rest of us, but to _____ it is. We will have five objects in all, and we will have a good idea of what our children think is important in this kind of emergency.

Let us see what we have today. Oh, look at this (hold up object). Tell us why you brought in this object.

Remember, Jesus is going away; we are filling this suitcase so when we are alone we will be all right. This is a good choice. I am a little surprised; I wonder how many of you would have chosen _____ (name object). We will add it to our collection. Who will add to the suitcase for next week? (Pick a volunteer.) I can hardly wait to see what it will be. What will be important?

Fourth Sunday of Easter

Gospel Lesson: John 10:11-18
Key Word: **I**
Object: ?

A gain I have a word for this lesson but no object. Today even the word is strange. It is the pronoun *I*. In this Gospel lesson Jesus uses the word "I" thirteen times. If we used that little word that often in just a few short passages people would say, You sure do talk about yourself a lot. That is not a good reputation to have. Our friends do not like us to talk about ourselves all the time. If you opened the Bible so you could see this lesson you would notice every time Jesus says I it is a capital I. Here is a little lesson for all of us to listen to about the letter I. The reason the I is a capital in the lesson is because it refers to Jesus or God, just like father always starts with a capital F when it refers to God. Here is the strange part: Every time you use the word I it is a capital letter. Some of you know this already, but do you know why? I just discovered the reason behind this, and now you will know too. Before we had the printing press everything was written in long hand. When words were printed, if the writer used a small *i* it got lost or stuck to another word. To make the poor little *i* stand out and not get lost they made all *I*'s capitals. I never knew that, did you?

Let us now talk about the thirteen I's in our lesson. This is the famous good shepherd Gospel. Jesus uses so many I's because he is telling us, I will take care of you. I know you. I will be with you when we meet my Father. I will die for you; I will rise to save you. That is one big job for anyone, even Jesus. If he can do all that for me he can use thirteen I's anytime. I is not a bad word to use if you can deliver like Jesus did on all his promises.

Jesus is one Sunday closer to leaving us. Here is my suitcase. So far we have a _____ and a _____. Today we add one more object. Whose turn is it? Thank you. (Hold it up.) Now we have a _____ to add to our suitcase. Do you want to tell us why you want this when you are alone? Fine. Now who wants to contribute something next Sunday?

Fifth Sunday of Easter

Gospel Lesson: John 15:1-8
Key Word: **Abide**
Object: ?

H ave you noticed that the last few weeks two things have been happening? First, I do not have an object; I do not even know what it will be until the end of the story. Second, we are spending more time with our key word. The reason we are doing that is because the key words are simple words we all know, but when we take a close look at them we learn something new about them. So far we have used *fear, witnesses,* and *I,* an interesting one-letter word. This week our word is *abide,* a word we all have heard and probably have some ideas about what it means. The hymn "Abide with Me" is familiar to all of us. (Sing it, if possible, this Sunday.) I always thought abide meant "stay with." That makes sense. We say to Jesus, Stay with me. That is a nice thought. Before we look into the meaning of abide, let us go back to the Gospel lesson. Jesus uses a grapevine as his illustration. He is standing with his disciples, looking over the hills that are covered with vineyards. The hills are cut into steps with row after row of grapevines. These vines were very large and very old. They had one root that could be eight or ten inches thick. From that one root three or four vines would shoot off in different directions. The man who owned the vineyard stretched the vines out on the ground so all the grapes would get some sun. Some of the vines were one hundred feet long. That is longer than from here to the back of the church. The man would look at each vine to see if it had dead branches or branches without grapes. These he cut off so the rest of the vine would grow stronger.

Jesus says, "I am the vine, you are the branches." We are to abide in him. We said abide means "to stay with" him. But no, now we find abide means "to live with" him. You live in your house. You are a member of a family. When you abide with Jesus you live with him.

You are not just a visitor; you are a member of the family. You may be all the way at the end of the one-hundred-foot-long vine, but you are tied to that root through the vine, and you abide or live attached to the root that is Jesus.

Jesus is going away. What do we have for our suitcase today? Bring it up so all can see. Now tell us why you picked this. Great! Into the suitcase it goes with our other things, so soon we will be ready to be left alone. I like the surpise each week of not knowing what the object is in my own object sermon. Will _____ bring in something next week?

Sixth Sunday of Easter

Gospel Lesson: John 15:9-17
Key Word: **Friend**
Object: ?

T his lesson continues from last week. This time Jesus is talking about the people he loves and the people who love him. He starts with our word from last week, *abide*: "Abide in my love." In fact he mentions it twice. You recall that abide in my love means "live in my love." That is real love when you live in it, not just get near it. The next thing Jesus says is really great. "You are my friends." Our word today is *friend*. As Jesus went about preaching, many people heard him and believed his message. Many of these people were not rich or powerful men and women, they were mostly slaves and servants. The message Jesus had that you could be free in Christ sounded better to slaves and servants than it did to the rich people. They were already free. Jesus said to the slaves and servants, If you love me, you are friends.

Let me tell you what this meant to those people. In those days if you were a wealthy person you could travel in any area that was part of the Roman Empire. When you traveled from town to town you might be stopped by the tax collector or robbers and beggars. It didn't matter who stopped you—you could take out a letter from the emperor that said you were a friend of the emperor, and the people ran away in fear because this meant you had power.

The slaves and servants who followed Jesus knew all about the friends of the emperor. Jesus was saying to them, Here is something for all of you. If you love me, you can say, I am a friend of Jesus, I am a friend of the King. The poor people understood what Jesus was saying. This was big news. Nobody ever said to them, You are no longer slaves or servants, you are my friends.

Jesus had something else to say to his new friends that was hard for some of them to do. Jesus said, "Love one another." Here are the slaves and servants, all friends of Jesus. That was easy, but now the servant who had a much better job than the slave was to love him. Jesus sure has a way of making things hard for us. This is for us today. If we love Jesus, he is our friend and we have to love the one who never takes a bath, we have to love the tough kid who always picks on everybody, and also the one with a different color skin than ours. We have to love the person who borrows our toys and forgets to return them. Your parents have to love the boss who is mean to them and that person who borrowed money and never returned it. Jesus said, "This I command you, to love one another." This command is for all people, not just the nice ones.

Bring up our last object and tell us why you think we should have it in our suitcase for the lonely time that is coming. Now we have all the objects; when Jesus leaves us we will be ready.

Seventh Sunday of Easter

Gospel Lesson: John 17:11-19
Key Word: **Sanctify**
Object: Suitcase with objects

W e are at the end of our children's sermons of Easter. A strange series—I had words, you had objects. We started by saying Jesus was going away and that we would be alone. Objects were brought in that we wanted with us when we were alone. For each of the past five weeks someone brought in an object that was important to them. The suitcase is filled with the five different things. We are all ready in case we find ourselves alone for a while.

I would like to tell you about our word for today before we get to the suitcase. It is *sanctify*. Does anyone know what it means? It is sort of hard. It means "set apart or separated." It is interesting that for the past five weeks we have been filling our suitcase to get ready to be left alone, and here on the last Sunday of Easter our word is sanctify which means "separated or set apart," and that is just what we have been talking about. Jesus says, "Sanctify them in the truth; thy word is truth." I wonder what that means. *Sanctify* is an old Hebrew word that you may not have heard before, but I will give you another Hebrew word I am sure you will know: *holy*. If sanctify means "separated," what do you think holy means in Hebrew? It means "set apart or separated." How about that, it means the same thing.

God is holy. In the Hebrew nation to be holy meant to be separated from the world that is full of sin. Jesus says "They are not of the world, even as I am not of the world." Separate them from the world in the truth. Whoever thought this would turn into a Hebrew lesson? Sanctify and holy both mean "separated."

Let us take a look at our suitcase. Jesus is going away; he is preparing his disciples and us for his departing for a while. In this suitcase are some very important items we will need if we are alone. Let us take a look. So many good things. I like them all. You put a lot of thought into what you brought. My suitcase is full of objects. You helped me; I only had words. I think before I close this suitcase I will put my words in also. They may prove to be a great help when we are alone.

Remember with me (have six pieces of paper each with one of the words on it). First week, *fear*; we are not afraid. Second week, *witnesses*; you are witnesses. Third week, *I*; Jesus says, "I am with you." Fourth week, *abide*; we live with Jesus. Fifth week, *friend*; he is our friend. Sixth week, *sanctify*; he set us apart. Now we can close our suitcase; it has everything we will ever need if we are alone. We will never have to be afraid, Jesus is with us as a friend forever.

Pentecost

(Series One—Fourteen Sundays

P entecost, also called Whitsunday, is a major festival in the Christian church. It is celebrated on the Sunday that falls after the fiftieth day after Easter Day and commemorates the descent of the Holy Spirit on the disciples after the death, Resurrection, and Ascension of Jesus Christ.

This long season for this book has twenty-seven Sundays, which have been divided into three series. The first is fourteen Sundays. These fourteen Sundays will be based on the sections of a major Sunday edition of a newspaper. If you get a copy of any big city Sunday paper, tear out the fourteen pages or sections listed below and place each in an envelope with the corresponding number on the outside. You need to give this envelope to a child each week and have it brought back to you when you ask for it.

Objects Required

☆ front page
☆ food section
☆ puzzle page
☆ garden page
☆ weather map
☆ obituaries
☆ society page
☆ travel section

☆ leisure section
☆ editorials
☆ employment
  or jobs section
☆ book reviews
☆ comics
☆ sports page

The Holy Trinity

(First Sunday after Pentecost)

Gospel Lesson: John 3:1-17
Key Word: **News**
Object: Front page of a newspaper

F or a few weeks we will be talking about what can be found in the Sunday newspaper. I have one right here. See how big and thick it is. I guess to read it all would take a long time. If you started now you might not finish until tomorrow.

We are not going to try to read all of the paper today. What we will be doing is looking at one page at a time to see how it relates to today's Gospel lesson. Our word today is *news*. I will use the front page of this newspaper because that is where the big news can be found.

Before we read the paper let us take a look at the Gospel lesson to see what the big news story is for today. Who can remember what the story was? Let me try to help a little. If you took all of the New Testament and put it into one sentence, that sentence was in our Gospel lesson today. If that could be done you would have done the job of the person who works at the newspaper who is called the headline writer.

(Hold up paper.) See the big headlines and all these smaller ones? They tell you what the article is about so that you can decide if you want to read it. Within our Gospel lesson is the sentence that would be the big headline on the front page of every Bible.

I will give you another hint—it is John 3:16. Does that ring a bell with anyone? Here it is: "For God so loved the world that he gave his only Son, that whoever

67

believes in him should not perish but have eternal life."

That is the big headline for today. We put up a headline that tells the story and makes people want to read more. It tells people everything you read in this story will lead you right back to this headline.

Did you ever notice when you look at the front page it seems to have all the bad news that is unfit to print. Not in our paper. We have all the good news that is fit to print. As we start our newspaper series for Pentecost we start wih the best news and the best headline. "For God so loved the world that he gave his only Son, that whoever believes in him should not perish but have eternal life."

Second Sunday after Pentecost

Gospel Lesson: Mark 2:23-3:6
Key Word: **Eat**
Object: Food section of newspaper

W hen I read the New Testament, I get the feeling that Jesus got into a disagreement with the leaders of the temple no matter where he went or what he did.

In this case there were thirty-nine laws to tell people what could not be done on the Sabbath. Three of the laws said you could not pick grain, you could not clean the grain, and you could not bake bread on the Sabbath.

As Jesus and the disciples walked through this field the disciples were hungry, so they picked some grains of wheat and ate them. The Pharisees took one look at them and said to Jesus, "Your disciples are breaking the laws of the Sabbath by picking and eating food."

If this had happened to us we probably would say, "Come on now, what's the big deal? These guys are hungry; should they starve or faint from hunger in order to keep a strange law like that?" Jesus did not even bother to argue with these men, instead he quoted the Old Testament story about David, who ate the show loaves of bread from the altar. These loaves were symbols left on the altar of the temple to remind the people of God's goodness. The difference between the disciples' eating on the Sabbath because they were hungry and David's eating was that the priest gave David the bread to eat. That made breaking the law acceptable.

Where is the newspaper for today? Look at all the food for sale! They even have desserts and cookies advertised. Suppose your mother was so busy she could not get to the store to do her food shopping and on Sunday she said, "I did not make it to the store, so today we do not eat. We will take a ride so you can forget how hungry you are." While riding you saw a store that was open, then a bakery, then an ice-cream stand, but you kept on riding past because your mother said you could not shop on Sunday. That might make sense to your mother, but your rumbling, hungry, stomach will not understand this one bit.

Perhaps that is how the disciples felt when the Pharisees picked on them for eating on the Sabbath when they were so hungry.

Jesus answered the Pharisees by explaining what God meant by that law. Jesus said: "On the sabbath we worship God; we show him how much we love him. The sabbath is a day of rest, when we think of all the blessings God has given us. This day was made for people to serve God, not to suffer or be hungry." Laws like the thirty-nine laws that tell what you cannot do on the Sabbath can help people, but when the laws become more important than the day itself Jesus strikes down the laws and says, Try love.

Third Sunday after Pentecost

Gospel Lesson: Mark 3:20-35
Key Word: **Forgiven**
Object: Puzzle page from newspaper

O h boy! That was some Gospel lesson for today. Remember during this Pentecost season we are starting with different sections of a newspaper. After listening to that lesson, what section do you think we should use today? May I have the envelope with the paper in it, please? I do not think you would guess, so I will show you. The puzzle page.

Do you think that is a good choice for the lesson? It surely is a puzzle. I suppose most of you have at one time or another worked on a puzzle. There are jigsaw puzzles for small children. There are word puzzles where you keep adding a letter until a word is spelled. Of course, there are crossword puzzles. Here is the puzzle in the paper. If you are good at these puzzles you can finish if you work hard enough. Some of us never finish one of these crossword puzzles. Sometimes we get so angry when we cannot find the right word we just give up; then along comes someone else, picks up the paper, and puts in words that we had been trying to find. It was easy for them. We get angry because the word was right there in front of us and we could not see it.

70

That is exactly what happened in the Gospel lesson. The scribes were really trying to find the truth about how Jesus performed miracles. These were not bad men; it was their job to see that if a person performed a miracle it was God's miracle. They also believed the devil could do miracles.

Here is the puzzle Jesus gave them to figure out. You say I am possessed by the devil. If I am and I get rid of the devil in other people, then I am working against myself. See, the devil does not beat the devil out of the devil! The devil fights God, and God fights the devil.

Jesus tells the scribes that if they see these miracles and think it is the work of the devil, they have the answer to the puzzle. It cannot be the devil. When you complete the puzzle you will see the miracles come from God.

Jesus says, I will forgive any sin except if you say, I am not God. Then he adds the final words to our puzzle. The words are, "If you say I believe, you will be saved." *Forgiven* is the last word of our puzzle and our word for today.

Fourth Sunday after Pentecost

Gospel Lesson: Mark 4:24-34
Key Word: **Seed**
Object: Garden page from newspaper

T oday we have two garden stories. The first tells us that when we plant a seed we have to be certain the soil is good. We have to water the seed and give it some food. We must do all the right things to help the seed grow into a strong plant. After we have done all that we can to be sure the seed will grow, we are done. There is nothing more we can do; now it is God's turn. He will not do our job, we have to do it; but when our job is done he takes over. We do not know why when we plant two seeds one will grow big and strong and the other never bears any fruit. We do not know what happened. God does.

Who has our newspaper for today? Here is the garden page in today's paper. You know what else they could call this page according to our Gospel lesson? They could call it God's little helper. This page tells us how and what to do to make a plant grow. It does not tell us how it happens, just how we can help God do his part in making the plant grow.

I do not see any mustard seeds for sale on this page. People do not plant mustard seeds as much as they used to. The mustard seed is not the smallest seed, but in the Bible they used this tiny seed to illustrate what a small thing could become. And this is our word for today—*seed*. In one summer this seed will grow into a tree with big, thick, strong branches. It can reach a height of twelve feet in just one season. In the holy lands every mustard tree had a nest of little birds called finches. There we have the mustard tree, starting out as a tiny seed, growing into a tree in one summer, feeding people and sheltering a family of finches.

This garden page helps us plan and plant our garden; then God makes it grow.

God is telling us through these stories that we have a job to do if all the people of the world are going to learn about Jesus. We should not be impatient; if we do our job, God's kingdom will come.

You young people are the plants that are growing in

God's garden. Your mothers and fathers must tend to these plants so that in God's good time they will mature and bear much fruit.

Fifth Sunday after Pentecost

Gospel Lesson: Mark 4:35-41
Key Word: **Storm**
Object: Weather map and report from the newspaper

C ould I have my paper now, please? In a few minutes we will find out what is in the envelope.

I remember one night when I was young and at home alone. It was a nice spring evening. The flowers were just starting to bloom, and you could smell their scent in the air. My parents had to go out for a while and they said I would be all right alone. I went out on our front porch and sat down. After a while I noticed some strange black clouds in the western sky. They seemed to be heading right toward my house. I did not like the looks of them, so I went in the house and thought that maybe they would just go away.

When I walked into the living room the evening paper was still open on the sofa, where my father had left it. It was open to the weather map (take paper from envelope). Under the map was the report for that day. It said it was to be fair and warm, today, tonight, and tomorrow. Chance of rain, zero. That made me feel better. I looked out the window; the big black cloud was now right over us. I looked again at the paper, and just then the loudest thunder and the brightest lightning I ever saw lit up the whole sky. I jumped in fright and hollered at the paper, you liar! Then the *storm* hit. I was so scared I did not know what to do. If Jesus had been there and said to me, "Why are you afraid?" I would have replied, "Because of your storm, that is why I am scared."

Sometimes when we read these Gospel lessons the message is so clear and simple. This one is so easy to understand every person in church today can understand it. Sometimes we naturally feel sorry for the poor disciples and think, It sure is easy for Jesus to stay calm; he is God.

If Jesus had said to me, in the middle of that storm, "Have you no faith?" I would have said, "I am so scared I can't even remember what faith is." What happened to that weather report? How could it be so wrong?

You know God works in strange ways to teach us who is in charge. Right at the height of the storm our telephone rang. You are not supposed to answer the phone in a lightning storm, but I did. My mother said, "Don't be afraid, we will be right home." Right then her voice chased all the fear out of me. I watched for them from the window. The lightning now was making the most beautiful blue designs in the sky, and my fear of the storm was gone.

The car pulled up with my parents in it and they ran into the house. My mother hugged me and asked if I was afraid. I said, Only for a little while.

We all need to hear that voice that we know and trust when we are afraid. It says, Do not be afraid, I am here.

Sixth Sunday after Pentecost

Gospel Lesson: Mark 5:21-43
Key Word: **Dead**
Object: Obituaries from newspaper

M ay I have the envelope please? Every newspaper has an obituary column, sometimes even a whole page. Let me show you the obituary page and tell you what it is all about. When people die something is written about what they did while they were living. Mr. So-and-So was a member of these clubs, this church, he leaves two sisters, one brother, three children, and four grandchildren. He died on such and such a day, burial will be tomorrow. Send money, no flowers. That is about how it goes. The person may have been eighty years of age, but they can sum up his entire life in two or three paragraphs.

For the past six weeks we have been looking at parts of a newspaper. This part is a little different. If the paper makes a mistake they can run a correction the next day. Maybe you have known instances where they will correct a statement from the day before—change the score of a ball game, for instance. There are no corrections on the obituary page. When you are *dead*, you are dead. That is our word for today.

Can you imagine what could have happened in Jesus' day if they had had newspapers and other fast ways to communicate like we do? The obituary would have read, "Jasmin, age 12, daughter of Jairus, one of the rulers of the synagogue, died in her sleep at home. Her mother was with her, her father was out trying to get a faith healer to come to help her. The father's efforts were too late. Please make gifts to the synagogue, Jasmin memorial fund.''

Let us forget for a minute that the obituary page is the only place in the paper where it is never wrong. Can you see the obituary page the next day? A big headline, "Oops, we were wrong! Jasmin, daughter of Jairus is alive again. The faith healer arrived too late; however, he said, 'Arise,' and she did! We regret this error, but we rejoice with Jairus and his family at this miracle.'' This has never happened before in the history of newspaper obituaries.

If you believe in Jesus, this obituary page is not the end. It is not perfect because we know death is not the end for those who believe. The newspapers would have to make corrections all the time if they believed as we do. Death is not the end; it is just the beginning of a new life with Jesus.

Seventh Sunday after Pentecost

Gospel Lesson: Mark 6:1-6
Key Word: **Honor**
Object: The society page from the newspaper

W ould you please bring me the newspaper? Today we are looking at the society page. I suppose there are not too many of you children who look at this page before you look at the comics or sports section. How many of you read the society page? Does anyone know what the society page is? Well, I am going to tell you about it.

In many places there are people who have money or

come from rich families. These people are good people just like us, except they have the time and money to travel and give dances and teas for charity. When they are married their pictures are in the paper. They are usually the leaders of the area. They are the ones you read about on the society page. We may even have some of them in our church. They are good people.

Now let me tell you who you will not see on the society page. If you were a poor carpenter with a big family, five sons and some daughters too, you probably would not make the society page. Poor carpenters do not fit in.

The Jewish nation had been waiting and waiting for the Messiah to come. They were certain that when he came he would be from one of those families that you would read about on the society page.

Listen to what happened. It is unbelievable. This poor carpenter's son, right from our own neighborhood, says he is the Messiah. No, he has not said it in so many words, but he certainly acts it. Does he really expect us to believe that he may be our Messiah? He is from the wrong side of town. He is not from a leading family. He is poor. We have known him since he was born. He is just a show-off and we won't take him too seriously.

You know to be a king you do have to come from a royal family. Jesus did not receive the honor that was due him. That is our word for today, *honor*.

This was the first time that Jesus was rejected. I imagine the first rejection hurt even more because it came from his own family and friends. You know how you have felt when you have done something well, really worked extra hard, then when you go home and tell your mother, I got an *A* on my test; but she is busy making dinner, Dad is reading the paper, and all you hear is,

"That's nice." You are so disappointed, nobody cares. We know that is not true, it is just that the world and people in it are too busy to give honor every time it is due.

Jesus accepted his rejection and went on with his ministry. He lived his whole life and died and never once made the society page. All he did was save the world.

Eighth Sunday after Pentecost

Gospel Lesson: Mark 6:7-13
Key Word: **Sent**
Object: Travel section of newspaper

Let us find out what is in our envelope. It is the travel section. This is one of my favorite sections to read, and I can dream about trips to China, Japan, Hong Kong. Going to the Orient has always interested me. There are trips to Europe and Africa that sound like fun too. I guess the trip I would really enjoy the most is the cruise on the Queen Elizabeth II. It is a trip around the world. This is only a dream because the cost of that trip would start at twelve thousand dollars and could go as high as fifty thousand for the deluxe cabin. I figure if one is going to dream, dream big. Then there are those South Sea Islands with their strange sounding names— Pago Pago, Bora Bora, Tahiti. They sound romantic; you can just visualize the white sands and blue waters.

Our word for today is *sent*. In the Gospel lesson, Jesus sent his disciples on a trip. They went two by two. In those days people almost always traveled with someone and carried a staff, so that if they met up with a robber they would not be alone and could defend themselves if attacked.

The trips Jesus had in mind for his disciples had very little to do with the nice deluxe trips and beautiful places we just talked about. There was no travel agent to make the arrangements. These men were not even certain where they would be going. Jesus told them to go, stop in each town, take no food or money or extra clothes. They were to go to the center of town or the temple and preach the good news, heal the sick, and help the people of the town in any way they could.

If the people did not want to listen to what the disciples had to say, they were to move on. Some would listen, take them in for the night, and give them food. The disciples were to tell them how to live. If you show people that you are willing to sacrifice for what you believe, then they will believe too.

We have now talked about two different kinds of trips. The one from the travel section is first-class. Fun all the way. Interesting, relaxing, and even educational. The other is tough, dangerous, and does not sound like much fun. I tell you if they advertised Jesus' trip in the travel section there would be few people anxious to go along.

Jesus asks us still to take a trip with him. It will be hard sometimes because we have to do things differently from the way other people do. We do not have to starve or fight off robbers, but we do have to be different.

When we finish our trip we will not have a lot of slides to show. We will know we took our trip Jesus' way, and we will feel as if we just had that fancy deluxe trip. Jesus is the best travel agent you will find; every trip is guaranteed.

Ninth Sunday after Pentecost

Gospel Lesson: Mark 6:30-34
Key Word: **Rest**
Object: Leisure section of newspaper

R est, our word for today, is a great thing, and we sure do need some once in a while. Rest means "ease after work." Isn't that interesting? If you do not work you cannot rest. I guess rest after rest is just called being lazy. Remember last week Jesus sent out the disciples two by two to preach and to heal. They have all returned and they need a rest. Jesus has the answer. He tells them they can get away from the people if they get into a boat. In the newspapers we have been discussing for weeks, there is even a section for this. May I have the envelope, please?

I think it is interesting that the leisure section of the paper comes only on Friday. That is the time we usually have a little time to rest. First we work all week, then we get a time to rest.

Jesus and his disciples got in the boat and headed down the lake for some rest and quiet. When the people saw them they ran along the shore and followed the boat. When the boat came onto the shore, the people came running up to Jesus. Jesus had compassion on them. That means "he felt sorry" for them. He knew they had followed him; they were tired and hot, and he did something we see happen all the time.

Did you ever see someone who loves his job? It may be your dad, or especially your mother. She can be very tired and needing a rest. She may sit down and say, "I am tired, I'll relax." All of a sudden she will remember that she promised to make a cake for the school fair. So she rushes into the kitchen and starts mixing and sifting, maybe even singing, as if she were not even tired. Your mother loves her job and she loves her family. When a job needs doing, tired or not, she gets a new strength and gets the job done. That is what happened to Jesus.

The boat pulled onto the shore. The big crowd was waiting, and all of a sudden he was no longer tired. He loved to help people. He loved to teach. He was full of new energy and eager to go.

Next week we will find out how Jesus' new energy allowed him to do his job of teaching. We will also see how he showed compassion for the people who followed him.

Tenth Sunday after Pentecost

Gospel Lesson: John 6:1-15
Key Word: **Sign**
Object: Editorials

O ur word for today is *sign*. That word comes right out of our Gospel lesson for today: "When the people saw the sign which he had done. . . ." In the Bible a sign is often a miraculous occurrence. Now can you see why we picked this one word out of the whole Gospel lesson to be our key word? What page shall we use for this lesson; what's in the envelope? It is the editorial page. I wonder if anyone has an idea what the editorial page has to do with the feeding of the five thousand? Is that a tough question? Do you know what the editorial page is?

The man who decides what will be printed in the paper is known as the editor. He has a big job. He writes a column every day and can say anything that is on his mind. It may be serious or funny, it is just what he feels that day. The editorial page is a very important page. In a news story the editor is not to let his opinion show. In the editorial it is all his opinion.

Jesus was not an editor, and he did not have a newspaper to print what he said. If he wanted to say something and make certain people noticed and remembered, he used a sign or a miracle. The people never forgot these times. They went home and told their friends about the great man they met who performed miracles. Now notice how all this ties together.

First, Jesus wanted a rest. Then he had compassion, he felt sorry for the crowd that had followed him. He started to teach them, and he wanted to be certain they never forgot his message. He wanted them to know that anything is possible for Jesus. He did not just say it, he used a sign, a miracle.

Jesus took five loaves and two fish. He blessed them, broke them, and served them to the crowd. There was food enough for everyone, with plenty left.

This was the way Jesus wrote an editorial. It was what was on his mind that day. He wanted to say, I have compassion for people, I can do anything. He performed the miracle of feeding those five thousand with five loaves and two fish. This showed he cared and that with Jesus all things are possible. Jesus wrote the editorial that day. The message was so strong that we still remember it two thousand years later. Boy, that is some editorial!

Eleventh Sunday after Pentecost

Gospel Lesson: John 6:24-40
Key Word: **Work**
Object: Employment section of newspaper

J esus was a traveling preacher. He very seldom preached to the same people more than once or twice. Two weeks ago there was a crowd that formed, so Jesus took his disciples off for a rest. The crowd followed, and Jesus performed the miracle of feeding the five thousand. This crowd is still following Jesus. It is almost like a treasure hunt. Jesus goes into hiding, the crowd follows and finds him. The problem Jesus is having with this group is that they do not seem to understand what Jesus is talking about. The reason we know they did not understand was because they came to him and he said, "You come to me because you want more bread." They missed the miracle of the five loaves and two fish. They saw five thousand people fed from so little and said, "This is like the old days, manna from heaven every day, no more work, no more hunger, just like the old days with Moses."

You must have heard some adults talk about the good old days. At the time they never seemed that great, but when we think back we always call them the good old days. The forty-years wandering in the desert was never the good old days, but now the crowd said that to Jesus.

Where is our newspaper section for today? Thank you. Look, it is the employment section. This is how you find a job if you want to work. That is our word for today, *work.*

Jesus tries to explain to these people what is important in life. He told them, "You came to me for free bread so you would not have to work for it. You do have to work, but save time to do the work of God." The people wanted to know what that was. Jesus said, very simply, "The work of God is to believe in God and believe in me." The people still wanted to argue with Jesus. They were still thinking about bread that is eaten. "Give us this bread always," they said.

By this time Jesus was wondering what he had to do to make the crowd understand what he was saying. He finally made it so clear there was no way not to understand. Jesus said, "I am the bread of life; he who comes to me shall not hunger, and he who believes in me shall never thirst." (Hold up paper.) See all these jobs? You know also the jobs your parents have; they are important. Jesus says, "This is the work of God, that you believe in him whom he has sent." That is God's work for you.

Twelfth Sunday after Pentecost

Gospel Lesson: John 6:41-51
Key Word: **Written**
Object: Book review section of newspaper

M any of the people who are arguing with Jesus in our Gospel lesson today are the same ones who have been following him for weeks. Most of the crowd have gone home, but there is still a group with him. Some are trying to understand and learn; others are trying to trip him up or prove him wrong.

Where is our newspaper for today? Look at this, it is the book review section. What in the world does the book review have to do with a group of people arguing with Jesus? Last Sunday they were arguing with Jesus, and today they continue to argue about the same thing. Remember what they used as the proof for the argument last week? A book. Not just any book but the Old Testament. They were giving Jesus a book review of the Old Testament. They said, it says this or it says that, as if Jesus did not know every word that was *written*, and this is our key word for today.

Because of what is written, now we begin to see more and more that most of these people were there not to learn but to try to trick Jesus with fancy words. Jesus is always ready to give them an answer because he is not doing a book review; he is the living fulfillment of the Old Testament.

In the lesson today Jesus said, "I am the bread which came down from heaven." Jesus at this time is not too far from his hometown. Many of these people know who he is. How can he say he came down from heaven when they know he is the son of Joseph, the carpenter from Nazareth? They ask him to prove to them that he is the Son of God by doing another miracle. Then Jesus says, "I am the living bread which came down from heaven; if anyone eats of this bread, he will live for ever."

There you have it—that is the miracle. If I eat of this bread, I live forever. That is hard to believe. I would like to have something easier to believe. Heal somebody or do something that I can see. Jesus says, "The bread is my flesh."

That was the last straw. Such an awful thing to say. I asked for a miracle, not a horror story. The people could not understand what Jesus was saying, they only listened to the words.

This book review is not going too well. Stay tuned for next week to see how it all comes out.

Thirteenth Sunday after Pentecost

Gospel Lesson: John 6:51-58
Key Word: **Live**
Object: Comics

T his whole series of Gospel lessons is getting a little out of hand. Here we have a group of people who keep arguing with Jesus, and the less they are able to understand, the more Jesus explains. The more he explains, the more he offends them. The crowd is smaller as we start our story. Where is our paper? Thank you. Look, the comics! It seems to me Jesus is talking about some very serious things to have the comics here to help us understand what he is saying. Let's see, here is what I wanted. "It's a bird, it's a plane, it's Superman." Did you hear the Gospel lesson? I wonder what Superman has to do with this whole series of arguments Jesus had with the people in our Gospel lesson?

Do you know the Superman comic that you see today in the paper and comic books and even in the movies began a long time ago? When I was young and first saw Superman, do you know what he used to do? He would fly, through wooden walls and even brick walls. He could hear through walls or even across the street, but not as well as he can today. The things that Superman did years ago that I thought were so great, you children today would think were pretty simple. After all, you have seen men walk on the moon, the space shuttle, and laser beams that carry sound; so Superman has to be able to do more than he did when I was young. As we get smarter Superman has to perform better tricks of strength or we will lose interest and go on to another comic strip that is up-to-date.

The more the people questioned Jesus, the more he tried to explain, and the less they understood. These people who had been with Jesus for quite a while still were only hearing the words and missing the message.

When you watch Superman, if all you see is his ability to fly over tall buildings, to stop cars going fast, to pick planes out of the air, then you do not know what Superman is all about. Superman came from Crypton to earth to show that good will always triumph over evil. Everything he does says just that.

Our word for today is *live*. Jesus came to say, "If you believe in God and you believe in me, you will never die, you will live for ever. Good will always triumph over evil."

Do not be like the people who followed Jesus in our lesson. Do not just hear the words, get the message too.

Fourteenth Sunday after Pentecost

Gospel Lesson: John 6:59-69
Key Word: **Disciples**
Object: Sports page of newspaper

I remember when our high school basketball team won the state championship. Some of us were not at the game; we listened to it on the radio. We were so excited when we won. We wanted to do something for the team. My mother had an old bed sheet and on it we painted, Welcome Home, Champs! We nailed this big sign over the front door of the school so that when the team returned they would know we were with them. The bus carrying the team finally pulled up at the school. A photographer from the local paper was there, and he took a picture of the team with their trophy in front of our sign. The picture was on the first page of the sports section of the paper, and we who had made the sign felt a part of the victory.

Where is my newspaper page? Thank you. Surprise! It is the sports page. This is the page for winners. When a team is winning, the stands are always full of fans. Tickets are scarce, usually a sellout. Everybody loves a winner. Just let the team hit a losing streak, however. If the championship team from last year goes on a ten-game losing streak, there are headlines in the paper reading, Fire the Manager, Get Rid of Some Players, Make a Trade. Do Something, We Cannot Stand a Loser. What a fast turnaround. It only takes a few weeks in most sports to lose ten games. The radio, newspaper, and TV reporters are upset. The stands are half full, and you can get a ticket anytime, if you want to see a loser. If you think you are disappointed, think how the team feels, how the manager feels. *Disciples* is our word for today. Disciples is another word for follower or fan. Some fans remain loyal through a losing streak. But many fans lose interest.

Jesus and the twelve faithful disciples seemed to be on a losing streak in the lesson today. The crowd had left, many of the disciples had left also, and Jesus asked the Twelve, "Are you going to follow the crowd and leave me too?"

After all the problems Jesus had with this crowd, trying to make them understand his message, he must have been a little depressed and discouraged. As the crowd disappears, he turns to his closest followers for encouragement. He offers them a chance to leave if they want, "Do you also want to go away?" Peter answers with the words that wrap up this whole series: "Lord, to whom shall we go? You have the words of eternal life."

That is the answer of a winner. Jesus will make a comeback. The stands will be full again.

Next Sunday we will begin a three-week discussion about, "Don't get so excited."

Pentecost

T his short series is a break after the long fourteen-week newspaper series. We will talk about hyper children, hyper parents, and hyper people in the Bible. Just as parents have to learn to deal with hyper and excited children, Jesus had the same problem with which to contend.

This should be a fun series because we are really at the children's level with these three objects

Objects Required
☆ regular cola, caffein-free cola
☆ regular coffee, decaffeinated coffee
☆ non-cola soft drink

Fifteenth Sunday after Pentecost

Gospel Lesson: Mark 7:1-8, 14-15, 21-23
Key Word: **Hyper**
Objects: Regular cola and caffeine-free cola

T oday for a change our word is not taken from the Gospel lesson. It certainly has to do with the lesson though. Our word is *hyper*. Can any of you tell me what that word means? (All right, that is good.) I guess your parents know its meaning because we have all experienced some stages of it at home. Hyper means, "over, above, more than normal," as in hyperactive. Now do you understand the word? We who have started to slow down sometimes think all children are a little hyperactive. You have so much energy! You never stop until you get into bed at night exhausted from a hard day. We get tired just watching you.

Now where is my soda boy and girl? Come on up, but you had better not shake the cans. We do not want a shower if the top should blow off. Do not be hyper. Here is a can (or bottle) of old-fashioned cola. This product has been made for years. It is the same old recipe. But now it has changed. This is caffeine-free cola. Caffeine makes you hyper, more active, so parents who had children who were active enough would usually decrease the quantity of cola their children wanted. Colas had to make a change after all these years. There is hope for us in this lesson; if colas can change, we can change.

In our lesson today we find our old friends the Pharisees, who were always watching everything Jesus did to try and trap him to prove they were right and he was wrong. Do you know what? Those Pharisees were hyper. They were like jack-in-the-boxes—waiting to pop out and tell Jesus, "You are wrong again." This did not bother Jesus because everytime they popped up he used it to teach a lesson.

We talked before about the many Jewish laws there were. Many laws were about how to wash and eat foods. Laws, laws, and more laws! The Pharisees saw some of the disciples skip a few of the laws and customs before they ate. The hyper Pharisees always hoped they would be able to say, We caught you. Jesus calmly answered them with a lesson and a new way to look at the old laws.

You will not get to heaven by washing your bodies or your food. It is not how you clean the things that you put into your bodies, it is what is in your heart and what comes out of a person that makes the difference.

Do not be hyper like the Pharisees and get carried away with all the unnecessary details. Be calm like Jesus, have a pure heart, all the rest will take care of itself.

Sixteenth Sunday after Pentecost

Gospel Lesson: Mark 7:31-37
Key Word: **Excited**
Objects: Regular coffee, decaffeinated coffee

I suppose not too many children drink coffee. Remember last Sunday we talked about cola, regular and caffeine-free. We said caffeine can make you hyper. Remember, that word means "over, above, more than normal." This week we have coffee. Will my coffee children bring me my coffee? Thank you. Here I have two cans of coffee. They both look the same, both taste the same, but there is a difference. This one is regular coffee; this is decaffeinated.

Have you ever gotten up in the morning and tried to talk to your mother or dad and they said, "Don't talk to me until I've had my coffee"? I remember when I was young I went into the kitchen and there was no one there, but the coffee pot was hot. I poured myself some coffee. I said, "Hello, hello," then I took a sip of coffee. It tasted awful. I was confused—why would they want to drink that peculiar tasting stuff? Now came the big test. I said, "Hello, hello." I thought I sounded exactly the same each time and wondered why I was never allowed to talk until they had their coffee—it does not make you talk any better or any different. Maybe it doesn't affect you until you get older. I learned later it is just the opposite at night. They say, "I do not want any coffee, I will not be able to sleep." This is very complicated; coffee makes you talk in the morning and keeps you awake at night.

Now we come to our word for today—*excited*. You get a little excited from the caffeine in this coffee (hold up regular). All that is changed; here is the answer, caffeine-free coffee. You still cannot talk in the morning until you drink it, but you can sleep at night.

In our Gospel lesson for today they were not drinking coffee to get excited. What excited them was something they saw, a miracle. A man was deaf and had a very serious speech problem. No one could understand a word he said. A terrible way to live. As Jesus came by, the people asked him to help the poor man. Sometimes Jesus was not certain if he was asked to heal because they believed that he could or because they just wanted to see a miracle. It was the best show in town. This time

Jesus took the man aside and very quietly healed him so the man could hear and speak. Talk about excited! The man was excited, the crowd was excited. They were all surprised at the miracle, and suddenly they saw what had happened. It was not just that this man could hear and speak, it was that God was here with them through his son Jesus.

It is great to be excited. When you are excited, do not miss the real miracle. It is not the show, it is that God is present. That is the miracle. He is here right now! I am excited about that. Are you?

Seventeenth Sunday after Pentecost

Gospel Lesson: Mark 8:27-38
Key Word: **Teach**
Object: Can of non-cola soft drink

T two weeks ago we had cola, and our word was *hyper*. Last week we had coffee, and our word was *excited*. Today we have a switch; we have a non-cola and our word is *teach*. Advertisements for non-colas boast on the fact that they have no caffeine.

By now we all know that caffein is not good for us. If I asked you to choose a soft drink that was best for you, which do you think it would be? Right, the non-cola. I am not telling you that you should drink sodas, but if you do it seems non-colas would be better for you.

Let us go back to our Gospel lesson. Jesus is talking with his disciples. He asked them the question, "Who do men say that I am?" The disciples said, "John the Baptist; and others say, Elijah; and others, one of the prophets." Then he turned to them and said, "Who do you say that I am?" Peter said, "You are the Christ." That is the real, pure thing. Nothing added, nothing artificial. The very simple pure truth, the real thing.

Our word today is *teach*. Jesus began to teach. We all know people who talk a lot. Even worse than that, some never seem to stop talking. Jesus was never like that. He knew he would have only three short years to prepare his disciples to start the church. He never wasted a word or a deed. He asked the question, Peter answered correctly, and Jesus began to teach. Many of us have had experiences with teachers, in school or at home. Teachers do not always say what we would like to hear. That is what happened here. Jesus tried to give his disciples a look at the future and they said, "We do not want to hear that."

Jesus became angry and told the disciples, "You must know what it will cost to follow me." The truth scared them. They wanted things to be the same. Jesus never missed a chance to teach. The lesson he left with his followers that day is just as important for us today. Follow the real thing, even if it costs something; maybe even your life.

Next Sunday we will start a series called *Start to Finish*. We will look at some things we eat every day and find out how they started.

Pentecost

(Series Three—Ten Sundays)

This last series will be a victim of Easter, the movable feast. You will use between five and ten of these sermons. Regardless of how many Sundays there are, do not forget the last Sunday after Pentecost (Christ the King Sunday) must be used as the final sermon of this series.

This series is called *Start to Finish*. We will use products like a peanut and then the finished product, peanut butter. The objects are simple things to show change from start to finish.

Objects Required

☆ peanut, peanut butter
☆ a piece of ripe fruit, piece of overripe fruit (apple)
☆ jar of mustard in a paper bag, hot dog and a roll in a bag
☆ sugar, candy
☆ flour, slice of bread
☆ handful of grass, glass of milk
☆ bunch of grapes, grape jelly, grape juice
☆ chocolate chips, chocolate chip cookies
☆ milk, butter
☆ butter, margarine

Eighteenth Sunday after Pentecost

Gospel Lesson: Mark 9:30-37
Key Word: **Child**
Objects: Peanut, peanut butter

H ere we go with our new series called *Start to Finish*. I will be showing you things you have in your house. Some things may be on the shelf where you keep groceries, others may be in the refrigerator. The past three weeks we talked about what makes you hyper; now we will be talking about what can make you healthy or fat or just happy.

Let us take a look at the Gospel lesson. The stories for this week and next are great stories for children. Jesus is talking about a *child*, our word for today, and he uses the child to show his disciples what it means to believe.

A child believes because he is told. This is true. That is the great thing about children, you believe what you are told. (Show the peanut.) Have any of you seen how a peanut grows? Let me tell you. It grows underground in a big clump. It has many roots. When you pull up the plant there are many peanuts growing in the roots. The root is often as big as a basketball, all full of peanuts. They are hidden underground. You cannot see them until you pull up the plant and then the plant is dead. The peanuts are green and have to be roasted before you can eat them.

This is what Jesus was trying to tell his disciples. The Son of man will have to die and be put in the ground and come out in three days. Then he will have completed his ministry on earth.

The disciples were so busy talking about themselves they did not understand how peanuts grow. They did not ask questions; they skipped over the plant's dying, the green peanuts, and the roasting. They were so interested in who was the greatest they almost forgot that Jesus was still with them. Do you know what they were doing? They were eating peanut butter (hold up jar). They forgot the steps it takes to make a peanut grow—they just went for the peanut butter. They did not care where it came from; they were afraid to ask.

Jesus is saying to us, all of us, First you plant, then it takes time to grow. When you pull up the plants, you pick the peanuts out of the roots, roast them, and then grind them into peanut butter.

Children, you are the little peanuts growing. You have a long way to go before you are peanut butter, but remember this: when Jesus wanted to say to his disciples, I will show you what it means to have faith, he took a child and said, "This is the best illustration of faith I know." A little child.

All my little peanuts, have faith and never lose it.

Nineteenth Sunday after Pentecost

Gospel Lesson: Mark 9:38-50
Key Word: **Sin**
Objects: A piece of ripe fruit (apple)
         A piece of fruit that is overripe (apple)

T he Gospel lesson for today is a continuation from last Sunday. Remember, we learned how children have faith or believe? Today Jesus warns us about what can happen if we teach a child not to believe. You may say to your friends, You do not have to be good to go to church school, You can disobey your parents and teachers, There is no God. But you know these things are bad and wrong.

When I was young I heard a story that illustrates this point so well. A father took his son and put him on a high stool and held out his arms to the boy and said, "Jump." Without a second thought the boy jumped, and his father moved away just as he jumped. The boy fell to the floor and started to cry, not because he was hurt but because he could not believe that his father had moved away and let him fall. His father told him to get up and stop crying, and then he said, "Let that be a lesson to you, never trust anyone, even your own father."

Jesus said that if you cause one of these little ones who believes in him to sin, (that means to lose faith in him), that is a sin, and it is your fault. That is our word for today, *sin.*

Look what I have here—a beautiful red apple. You can see just from looking at it that it is ripe and will be juicy. If I take a bite out of it, it will probably crack and spray some juice, just the way a good apple should. Oh my, look, I brought two apples with me today, and this one has some bad spots on it. It does not even smell good. What a shame. Once these apples looked and smelled and probably would have tasted alike. Something happened to this bad one. I do not want to eat it, do you? I guess the only thing to do with it is throw it away.

That is what the Gospel is telling us. We have a job to do with our friends and family. We have to watch the other apples around us and be sure none of them goes bad. You all have to do your part. If the apples you know go bad, help them. Help them to believe so they do not sin and like this poor apple (hold up the bad one) have to be thrown away. Help them to be strong and good like this good apple. That is what Jesus wants and that is what we like too, a lot of good apples.

Twentieth Sunday after Pentecost

Gospel Lesson: Mark 10:2-16
Key Word: **Receive**
Objects: Jar of mustard in a bag, hot dog and roll in a bag

For the last two weeks we have been talking about Jesus and what he thought about children. We found that he loved them very much, and we get the idea that he felt they were very special. He used children to teach older people about the kingdom of God. Today we come to his last lesson on children, and he makes it very clear why he loves them and how he uses children to teach his great lessons of faith and love.

Everyone should listen to this children's sermon. It will apply to all. Our word for today is *receive*. That is an easy word. Who can tell me what it means? That is very good. I will tell you what the dictionary says, "To be given, to get, to take." Do you see why that is our word for today? Jesus says, If you do not get or take what is given as a child you will not receive the gift. Let us take a look at the message in the Gospel. In this bag I have something you might like to eat. I will tell you what it is and will leave one word out and I want you to decide if you would like to try this. It is vinegar, seeds, salt and other spices, and turmeric. I even have trouble pronouncing that last one. What I have done is take a very simple message and make it complicated. Remember I left out one word? Let me give you a clue as to the word I left out. (Uncover the hot dog on a roll.) A hot dog. What goes on a hot dog that sounds like—let me give it to you again—vinegar, salt, spices, turmeric, and some kind of seeds that we talked about a few weeks ago? Mustard seeds. (Open the bag.) It is mustard for our hot dog. That was the hard way of getting around to asking if you would like to have a hot dog with mustard. That is exactly why Jesus talks so much about receiving and believing as a child. Keep your faith simple.

When you say to a child, Ask Jesus to be with you when you go to sleep, that child knows Jesus will be there. That is the kind of faith the child has. Remember our story from last week about the father who said "Jump," and then let his son fall? Jesus will never step away and let you fall. You do not need to know what goes into mustard, just that a hot dog with mustard tastes great. So children, believe without question. Receive without question. No matter what your age, when you accept as a child, you will understand the message to all of us.

Twenty-first Sunday after Pentecost

Gospel Lesson: Mark 10:17-30
Key Word: **Possessions**
Objects: Sugar, candy

W hat is important in your life? Of all the things you own, what is the one thing you love most? Your dog, your cat, a toy, a bike? What is the one thing you would not want to give up no matter what happens?

(Get some answers from the children.) All of us have some things that are important to us. Our word today is *possessions*, a word taken from our Gospel lesson.

A young man came up to Jesus and wanted to know how he could inherit eternal life. That means going to heaven when he dies. Jesus is about to teach this young man a lesson, and that lesson fits us too. He told the young man to obey the commandments, which is the Old Testament law. The young man said, "No problem," he did that already. Jesus was pleased with that and then told him one other thing he would have to do. "Sell everything you have, give it to the poor, and follow me." Jesus and this young man were getting along just fine up to that time. I cannot figure out how Jesus does it, but he always seems to see right through us. He finds our weaknesses and then jabs us. This young fellow was very rich. He had money, land, cattle, much. He was a good man, but Jesus wanted one more thing from him and the man would not do it. He walked away from Jesus. His possessions came first, above everything else in his life.

Here I have some sugar. (Hold up a bag or bowl.) You know what we do with sugar. Name some things for me. We put it on cereal or fruit, in tea or coffee, make cakes or cookies. Now if this was your sugar bowl and I asked you for a spoonful of sugar you would be only too glad to let me have some, wouldn't you? That would be the nice thing to do. Just like the young man who was talking to Jesus, you are a good person.

Now you take your sugar and go to the candy man and have him make a nice piece of candy for you. The candy man finally comes out with a piece of candy he made with your sugar (show a piece of candy). After the walk to the store, waiting patiently for the man to make your

102

candy, and smelling the good smells of the store, you are really ready to taste that candy. You are about to put it in your mouth and I come along and say to you, Can I have that piece of candy, please? You do not walk away from me like the young man walked away from Jesus; you pop the candy into your mouth and eat it saying, Too late, it is all gone. Sometimes we work so hard for something we want so much, it possesses us instead of us possessing it. Jesus says that is very bad. When you love your possessions more than your life you are in danger of losing everything.

Twenty-second Sunday after Pentecost

Gospel Lesson: Mark 10:35-45
Key Word: **Whatever**
Objects: Flour, slice of bread

D id you ever go to a movie or watch a television show and after it started you could tell how it was going to end? That is disappointing. You are all set for the mystery show, and in the first few minutes it is all over for you. Then suddenly something happens; it is not going to end the way you thought it would. It is not at all the way you had it figured out. Hey, this is getting interesting. I was all wrong, it is a great story. Am I glad I am watching this! When the show is over you are exhausted. It was great. What a finish! This happens to older folks too, not just children. I am going to tell you a secret. Do you know how to get your parents upset? Just say, "I want you to do whatever I ask." Your parents will never say yes. They've learned a few things about whatevers after all the years they have been around. Our key word today is *whatever*. That is the kind of word that often causes problems for parents. This time it got James and John in trouble.

Here is a cup with something in it. I need three children to help me. (Have them come up front.) Put a wet finger in this cup and taste this white stuff and see if you can tell me what it is. What did it taste like? Was it good, bad, or just awful? Remember now, on these Sundays we have things that end differently from the way they started out. What do we have here? Can anyone guess how it is going to end? Anybody else want to try? Now, I'll reach over and uncover the finished product. It is a piece of bread. You were eating plain flour. When you add other items and bake it, it becomes bread. It is like that mystery show that ended differently from what we thought. We did not know that the flour would turn into bread.

James and John said to Jesus, "We want you to do for us whatever we ask of you." It did not end the way they thought it would either. They still thought it was a big game, and they wanted to be a couple of big players. They told Jesus, "When you are king we want to be on your left and right." Jesus answered very quietly, "If you want to be great, you must be a slave or servant to your fellowman. If you want to do what I do, you must die with me." See, it was all mixed up again; James and John wanted to sit next to the king and all of a sudden they are told, "Be a slave and be ready to die." The whatever questions sure do end up differently than we think they will sometimes, don't they?

Twenty-third Sunday after Pentecost

Gospel Lesson Mark 10:46-52
Key Word: **What**
Objects: Grass, glass of milk

L ast week we talked about the question that James and John asked Jesus that has the word *whatever*. This week we see Jesus leave himself open to another problem by asking the blind man Bartimaeus, "What do you want me to do for you?" This is our word today, *what*. Last week we said that parents are too sharp to get caught in the whatever trap. Here is Jesus walking into the same kind of trap.

Let me show you a miracle. (Hold up a handful of grass.) What do I have in my hand? Can everybody see it? Come up if you can't and look at it. You know in the past few weeks I have had some strange things, so be careful of this. What is it? It is just plain grass that I pulled up on my way to church. I said "Just plain grass," but there must be more to it than that. Let us return to the Gospel lesson for a minute.

Bartimaeus was sitting by the side of the road. Sitting in the grass. Sitting on a miracle waiting for a miracle. This plain grass is part of a miracle that has been going on for years, and today, even with our modern technology, we have not been able to match this miracle. People have worked for years trying to build a machine to match this miracle; we have also tried to match it in laboratories with chemicals. It has never been done. Do you know what the miracle is? I will show you. It starts with the grass, now it is a glass of milk. The cow eats the grass and the cow gives us milk. That is a real miracle. No machine can make milk, it takes grass and a cow.

Remember earlier in this story we talked about Jesus leaving himself wide open by saying to Bartimaeus, "What do you want me to do for you?" Jesus was not worried that this man would ask him to do something he was unable to do; he wanted to know if this man was ready for a miracle. Remember the rich young man who was not ready for Jesus? Jesus tested him, and he failed the test. Now Jesus is giving another man another test. The question Jesus was asking was, You are blind, do you really think I can make you see again? Who do you think I am? The man answered, "Master." Do you know what master means? It is a man who has power or control. The man answered by saying, "You have the power, let me receive my sight." The man passed the test. He knew Jesus could do it. That is the kind of faith Jesus demands in exchange for his miracles. How do you think you would do if Jesus tested you?

Twenty-fourth Sunday after Pentecost

Gospel Lesson: Mark 12:28-34
Key Word: **Commandment**
Objects: Bunch of grapes, grape jelly, grape juice

Today I have a question for you. How many commandments did the Jewish people have, according to the Old Testament? Ten is correct. But the priests added a few just to make life more difficult.

When the scribes in our Gospel today asked Jesus, "Which commandment is the first of all?" That was not a tough question to answer if there were only ten. At that time in the history of the Jewish people they had 613 commandments. So you can see when Jesus was asked that question by the scribes it was a pretty tough question to answer.

Our word today is *commandment.* A commandment is a law. We have a hard time with ten; imagine how hard it would be with 613. Jesus was asked to pick one. He did, with no trouble. The first is, "You shall love the Lord your God . . . " and " . . . love your neighbor as yourself. . . ." It is not two laws, it is one split in half. You love God and man.

I will try to explain so you know what I mean. I have a bunch of grapes. These are all the laws and verses in the Bible that say you must love God. If you asked me to take these grapes and tell you which was the most important grape, I would take them and squeeze them until I had a big glass of juice (take out glass of grape juice). All the commandments and verses that say "love God" are now down to one. But Jesus did not say there is only one commandment, he said two. If I take this grape juice and add a few things like "love your neighbor," we still have the same juice but it is a little thicker because we added more love—and now what do we have? Jelly! (Hold up jelly jar.) Grape jelly.

We started with a bunch of grapes. We squeezed them and had grape juice and then grape jelly by adding more love.

Do you see what Jesus was doing? The scribes were trying to make life hard for the Jewish people with their 613 commandments. Jesus was trying to make live easier by saying only two, not 613. The scribes did not know how to answer Jesus because what he had said made so much sense. It really is quite simplc, love God, love man.

Twenty-fifth Sunday after Pentecost

Gospel Lesson: Mark 12:38-44
Key Word: **Contributing**
Objects: Chocolate chips and chocolate chip cookies

Our word today is *contributing;* it is from the Gospel. Do you know what it means? It means "not to just give, but to give along with others." Can you see the difference? You can give me a gift, and that is a nice thing to do. If you give money to your church or the United Fund you are not just giving, you are contributing because you are giving along with others. In the Gospel, Jesus never said the people gave money to the treasury, he said they contributed to the treasury. Jesus knew the difference.

The last part of our lesson is the story of the widow's mite. That means her little bit. The rich people gave large sums of money; they had large sums to give. The widow had only two copper coins worth about a penny. She contributed both of them. When she left the Temple she had nothing left. Jesus said, "That is a real gift, not what you can afford to give, but giving it all." One of those 613 commandments we talked about last week said, "You are to give ten percent of all you have." This is the first time Jesus tells us that is not enough. We are to give as we receive. From him who has much, much is expected, above and beyond the ten percent.

I have here a bag of chocolate chips. The bag is still sealed so I will not eat them, otherwise there would be nothing to show. I love chocolate chips. On the back of the package is a recipe for chocolate chip cookies, Toll-House cookies we used to call them, but now we call them chocolate chips. They are made of flour, salt, butter, sugar, vanilla, eggs, and brown sugar. Then you make a dough and roll out little balls that will flatten out in the heat of the oven and then you have—oops—we forgot to put in our bag of chocolate chips. To our big bowl of cookie dough we now add the little bag of chocolate chips. We have chocolate chip cookies.

Remember in our lesson the rich people put in large sums. Jesus was most impressed by the two copper coins put in by the widow. Remember when I read all the things that went into the cookie dough to make a big bowlful, then we put in the little bag of chocolate chips, and we called them chocolate chip cookies? That widow gave all she had because it pleased God. We call these chocolate chip cookies because it is those little chips that make these cookies great.

Life is full of a lot of little things that sometimes count more than the big things. Little things can contribute to make big things happen.

Twenty-sixth Sunday after Pentecost

Gospel Lesson: Mark 13:24-32
Key Word: **Learn**
Objects: Milk, butter

O ur Gospel lesson today is not one that lends itself easily to a children's sermon. After reading it a number of times, I was just about to give up when I saw the words ". . . the heavens will be shaken." Suddenly I thought of a miracle we talked about a couple of weeks ago.

I chose as our word for today, *learn*. "From the fig tree

learn its lesson." Let us see what we can learn today.

Back to our miracle of a few weeks ago. The miracle started with a handful of grass. That is right, milk. People have not been able to manufacture milk, only the cow can do that. Here is a glass of milk again (we should have had this to go with our cookies). I told you milk is a daily miracle. What I will show you today is not a miracle, it is a process that will take this milk and change it into something entirely different. Suppose I put this milk into a churn that mixed and shook the milk for about twenty minutes. What would happen? The milk would turn to butter. One thing I forgot to tell you, however: you cannot use ordinary milk because it is homogenized. That means the cream is mixed in with the milk. We would have to separate the cream from the milk. It is the cream that becomes butter.

In our Gospel lesson Jesus is talking about the end of the world. Everything will be shaken and mixed up. The milk and the cream will be separated. Someday, we do not know when, Jesus will come and sort out all the bad people. The good people he will call his own, and his kingdom will be here.

Christy the King

(Last Sunday after Pentecost)

Gospel Lesson: John 18:33-37
Key Word: **King**
Objects: Butter, margarine

T his Sunday is called Christ the King Sunday. In our Gospel lesson today, Jesus is meeting with Pilate in the Praetorium; that was the house where the Roman governor lived. It is now Holy Week. Jesus is a prisoner and on trial for his life. Pilate wants no part of this whole trial. He tries to give Jesus back to the Jewish authorities, but they will not take him. They tell Pilate that Jesus is his problem and Pilate must be the judge and pass the sentence. Pilate is looking for a way out. He brings Jesus into his home and talks to him. Pilate likes Jesus and thinks he is a gentle person, not a man who should be put to death as the priests wanted.

Pilate asked Jesus if he was the king of the Jews. Pilate expected him to say, No, I am not a king. After all, Pilate saw this gentle man standing with his hands tied behind him and he certainly did not look like a king.

Jesus said, "I am a king, but my kingdom is not of this world." Then he said, "I have come to bear witness to the truth." Jesus says, I am a king, not of a country but of truth.

For weeks now we have been talking about different foods. Here are two foods that are so much alike you cannot tell which is which by tasting them. Here is some butter (hold item up). Here is some margarine. This is made from corn oil; some say it is better for you than butter. They look the same and taste the same, but it is

111

not butter. The truth is, butter is butter and margarine is margarine.

Since Jesus stood before Pilate two thousand years ago a lot of people have said, I am the king, and a lot have said, I am the truth. There is only one true King, not of this world but King of truth forever. Christ the King.